T0247876

The Science of Addiction

Published in 2025 by Scientific American Educational Publishing
in association with **The Rosen Publishing Group**
2544 Clinton Street, Buffalo NY 14224

Contains material from Scientific American®, a division of Springer Nature America, Inc.,
reprinted by permission, as well as original material from The Rosen Publishing Group®.

First Edition

Scientific American
Lisa Pallatroni: Project Editor

Rosen Publishing
David Kuchta: Compiling Editor
Michael Moy: Senior Graphic Designer

Cataloging-in-Publication Data
Library of Congress Cataloging-in-Publication Data

Names: Scientific American, inc., editor.
Title: The science of addiction / the editors of Scientific American.
Description: First edition. | New York : Scientific American Educational
Publishing, 2025. | Series: Scientific American explores big ideas |
Includes bibliographical references and index. | Audience: Grades 10-12
Identifiers: LCCN 2024015509 | ISBN 9781725351721 (library binding) | ISBN
9781725351714 (paperback) | ISBN 9781725351738 (ebook)
Subjects: LCSH: Compulsive behavior–Juvenile literature. | Substance
abuse–Juvenile literature. | Compulsive behavior–Treatment–Juvenile
literature. | Substance abuse–Treatment–Juvenile literature.
Classification: LCC RC533 .S383 2025 | DDC 616.86–dc23/eng/20240415
LC record available at https://lccn.loc.gov/2024015509

Manufactured in the United States of America
Websites listed were live at the time of publication.

Cover: Viktoriya/Shutterstock.com

CPSIA Compliance Information: Batch # CSSA25.
For Further Information contact Rosen Publishing at 1-800-237-9932.

CONTENTS

INTRODUCTION

More than 100,000 Americans die every year from drug overdoses. Nicotine addiction results in 480,000 deaths annually. Some 178,000 Americans die every year from excessive alcohol use. Nearly 49 million Americans aged twelve or older have a substance use disorder, according to the 2022 National Survey on Drug Use and Health, split evenly between alcohol and drugs.

These are grim numbers. Addiction is a lethal problem, but it is also a complicated one. The science of addiction has moved beyond treating addiction as the personal failing of "weak" people to understanding it as a disease beyond the voluntary control of the person. Still, the stigma of substance abuse disorders plagues both society's view of addiction and often the treatment of it. Medical science can help us better understand what addiction is, how it differs depending on the substance abused, how it can be treated, and how we can prevent its worst outcomes.

In Section 1, we start by looking at how addiction is defined within medical science, in order to better identify it and its causes. In Section 2, we take a historical look at the origins and development of addiction science, featuring the pioneering work of Marie Nyswander. In Section 3, we turn to the epidemic of opioid addiction, as increasingly powerful—and increasingly addictive—drugs do both harm and good. Section 4 examines the contribution of medical science to how addiction is treated, and finally in Section 5 we look at how a better understanding of the prevalence and chemistry of overdoses can lead to new ways of preventing and reversing overdoses.

Addiction often feels like a grim competition between black hat chemists and white hat chemists, one group seeking to hook and harm, the other to help and heal. Many times it feels like the black hats are winning, which is all the more reason to profile the scientific breakthroughs and advances of those trying to fight these disorders.

Section 1: Defining Addiction

Is Addiction a Disease?

By Elly Vintiadis

The prevailing wisdom today is that addiction is a disease. This is the main line of the medical model of mental disorders with which the National Institute on Drug Abuse (NIDA) is aligned: addiction is a chronic and relapsing brain disease in which drug use becomes involuntary despite its negative consequences.

The idea here is, roughly, that addiction is a disease because drug use changes the brain and, as a result of these changes, drug use becomes compulsive, beyond the voluntary control of the user. In other words, the addict has no choice, and his behavior is resistant to long-term change.

This way of viewing addiction has its benefits: if addiction is a disease then addicts are not to blame for their plight, and this ought to help alleviate stigma and to open the way for better treatment and more funding for research on addiction. This is the main rationale of a recent piece in the *New York Times*, which describes addiction as a disease that is plaguing the U.S. and stresses the importance of talking openly about addiction in order to shift people's understanding of it. And it seems like a welcome change from the blame attributed by the moral model of addiction, according to which addiction is a choice and, thus, a moral failing—addicts are nothing more than weak people who make bad choices and stick with them.

Yet, though there are positive aspects to seeing addiction in this light, it seems unduly pessimistic and, though no one will deny that every behavior has neural correlates and that addiction changes the brain, this is not the same as saying that, therefore, addiction is pathological and irreversible.

And there are reasons to question whether this is, in fact, the case.

From everyday experience we know that not everyone who tries or uses drugs and alcohol gets addicted, that of those who do many

8

quit their addictions and that people don't all quit with the same ease—some manage on their first attempt and go cold turkey; for others it takes repeated attempts; and others still, so-called chippers, recalibrate their use of the substance and moderately use it without becoming re-addicted.

But there is also strong scientific evidence that most people recover from addiction on their own and that things are not as simple as the medical model implies.

In 1974 sociologist Lee Robins conducted an extensive study of U.S. servicemen addicted to heroin returning from Vietnam. While in Vietnam, 20 percent of servicemen became addicted to heroin, and one of the things Robins wanted to investigate was how many of them continued to use it upon their return to the U.S. and how many remained addicted. What she found was that the remission rate was surprisingly high: only around 7 percent used heroin after returning to the U.S., and only about 1-2 percent had a relapse, even briefly, into addiction. The vast majority of addicted soldiers stopped using on their own.

Also in the 1970s, psychologists at Simon Fraser University in Canada conducted the famous "Rat Park" experiment in which caged isolated rats administered to themselves ever increasing—and often deadly—doses of morphine when no alternatives were available. Yet, when these rats were given a mate and alternatives to drugs they stopped taking them. And in 1982 Stanley Schachter, a Columbia University sociologist, provided evidence that most smokers and obese people overcame their addiction without any help.

Although these studies were met with resistance, lately there is more evidence to support their findings.

In *The Biology of Desire: Why Addiction Is Not a Disease*, Marc Lewis, a neuroscientist and former drug addict, argues that addiction is "uncannily normal," and he offers what he calls the learning model of addiction, which he contrasts to both the idea that addiction is a simple choice and to the idea that addiction is a disease. Lewis acknowledges that there are undoubtedly brain changes as a result of addiction, but he argues that these are the typical results of neuroplasticity in learning and habit formation in the face of very attractive rewards.

In reviewing a number of case studies, Lewis argues that most addicts don't think they are sick (and this is good for their recovery) and that the stories of people who have overcome their addiction, instead of impotence and disease, speak of a journey of empowerment and of rewriting one's life narrative. That is, addicts need to come to know themselves in order to make sense of their addiction and to find an alternative narrative for their future. In turn, like all learning, this will also "re-wire" their brain.

Taking a different line, in his book *Addiction: A Disorder of Choice*, Harvard University psychologist Gene Heyman also argues that addiction is not a disease but sees it, unlike Lewis, as a disorder of choice. Heyman presents powerful evidence not only that just about 10 percent of people who use drugs get addicted and only around 15 percent of regular alcohol drinkers become alcoholics but also that around 80 percent of addicts overcome their addiction on their own by the age of 30. They do so because the demands of their adult life, like keeping a job or being a parent, are incompatible with their drug use and are strong incentives for kicking a drug habit.

This might seem contrary to what we are used to thinking. And, it is true, there is substantial evidence that addicts often relapse. But most studies on addiction are conducted on patients in treatment, and this skews the population sample. Most addicts never go into treatment, and the ones who do are the ones, the minority, who have not managed to overcome their addiction on their own.

What becomes apparent is that addicts who can take advantage of alternative options do, and do so successfully, so there seems to be a choice, albeit not a simple one, involved here as there is in Lewis's learning model—the addict chooses to rewrite his life narrative and overcomes his addiction.

However, saying that there is choice involved in addiction by no means implies that addicts are just weak people, nor does it imply that overcoming addiction is easy. It is incredibly hard, and for some people, practically impossible to undo years of habit.

The difference in these cases, between people who can and people who can't overcome their addiction, seems to be largely about determinants of choice. Because in order to kick substance addiction there must be viable alternatives to fall back on, and often these are not available. Many addicts suffer from more than just addiction to a particular substance, and this increases their distress; they come from underprivileged or minority backgrounds that limit their opportunities, they have histories of abuse, and so on. So although choices are in *principle* available, *viable* choices for people are largely dependent on determinants of choice beyond their control, and this can mitigate their responsibility.

This is important, for if choice is involved, so is responsibility, and that invites blame and the harm it does, both in terms of stigma and shame but also for treatment and funding research for addiction.

It is for this reason that philosopher and mental health clinician Hanna Pickard of the University of Birmingham in England offers an alternative to the dilemma between the medical model that does away with blame at the expense of agency and the choice model that retains the addict's agency but carries the baggage of shame and stigma. Both these models, Pickard claims, place the responsibility away from us: it is either the addict's fault or the disease's. But if we are serious about the evidence, we must look at the determinants of choice, and we must address them, taking responsibility as a society for the factors that cause suffering and that limit the options available to addicts. To do this we need to distinguish responsibility from blame: we can hold addicts responsible, thus retaining their agency, without blaming them but, instead, approaching them with an attitude of compassion, respect and concern that is required for more effective engagement and treatment. And the two, responsibility and blame, can come apart if we realize that responsibility is about the person who makes choices, but blame is about our choice of how to respond to them.

In this sense, the seriousness of addiction and the suffering it causes both to the addicts themselves but also to the people around them require that we take a hard look at all the existing evidence and at what this evidence says about choice and responsibility—both the addicts' but also our own, as a society. We can call addiction a disease because the concept of a disease is not clearly defined, but if by "disease" we mean that there are brain changes that lead to lack of choices, then there is ample evidence to dispute this view. In the end, we cannot understand addiction merely in terms of brain changes and loss of control; we must see it in the broader context of a life and a society that make some people make bad choices.

This article was published in Scientific American's *former blog network and reflects the views of the author, not necessarily those of* Scientific American.

About the Author

Elly Vintiadis teaches philosophy at the American College of Greece. Her main research is in the philosophy of mind, the metaphysics of mind and the philosophy of psychiatry.

Food, Sex, Gambling, the Internet: When Is It Addiction?

By Carl Erik Fisher

T heo did not seem like the type to become addicted to gambling. He was a literary star who had published his first novel at age 24 to great success. While traveling through Europe, he began visiting elegant casinos, at first dabbling in table games like roulette. With time, though, this pleasant diversion became a compulsion, and he lost nearly all his money in just a few years. He continued to produce critically acclaimed books—at one point churning out a new novel in less than a month to settle urgent debts—but he struggled to stay afloat, and his wife soon had to sell her jewelry. Remarkably, aside from the gambling, his life seemed fine. His writing was respected, and his family life was satisfying. He was simply hooked.

"Theo" is actually Fyodor Dostoyevsky, the prototypical gambling addict. Despite profound insight into the human condition, Dostoyevsky struggled with gambling for many years and was almost financially ruined several times. His semiautobiographical novel *The Gambler*—written to cover his debts, published in 1867—described compulsive gambling so well that 20th-century psychiatrists studied it as a model for the concept of gambling addiction.

Well over a century ago people already realized that an individual could have what is today called a behavioral addiction: an overwhelming, repetitive and harmful pattern of behaviors apart from drug or alcohol abuse. Now, 150 years after Dostoyevsky first walked into the casinos of Romantic-era Europe, addictions to sex, eating, video games and other behaviors are getting serious recognition in some quarters of medicine and among the public. Casualties of behavioral addictions are appearing in the news: not just gamblers throwing their life savings away but also porn addicts masturbating to iPhones on the freeway and even babies left to die by parents engrossed in video games. Doubters, however, argue that slapping the addiction label on these habits inappropriately excuses bad behavior.

Are these behaviors mental disorders? Many people are striving to limit their screen time or watch their diets, but does that mean that Internet and food addiction epidemics are upon us? Proponents argue, neuroscience evidence in hand, that behavioral addictions are brain disorders, but critics question those interpretations and protest that we are unnecessarily medicalizing everyday suffering.

This leaves psychiatrists like me in a difficult position. In my practice in New York City, I received more inquiries in the past year from people seeking help for Internet addiction than for cocaine and heroin addiction combined. It is hard to deny that for some of them, behavioral addictions are real—these individuals are truly overwhelmed by repetitive, harmful behaviors. Their schooling, marriage or job is in danger because of their uncontrolled actions. They sincerely want to stop, but they feel powerless. A mental disorder is defined simply as a dysfunctional thought process or behavior that causes harm. In my view, some behavioral addictions clearly meet that description—there is a reason we have had this intuition since the time of Dostoyevsky.

Yet many people rush to diagnose themselves with behavioral addictions, not recognizing the underlying depression or anxiety driving their problems. Treatment for them may have different considerations, and research is just starting to offer clues about how to help these different types of addictions. After all, that is the goal of all the questions and debates—how can we best help people who are suffering?

As I set out to understand this phenomenon, I found that even the experts within the field are divided—and that includes those who support the idea of behavioral addiction. But along the way I also caught glimpses of paths toward a resolution.

Disordered Desires

People were making unhealthy choices about sex, eating and money well before Dostoyevsky. Saint Augustine's *Confessions*, written sometime around the year 400, intricately explores loss of control over sexual impulses. The root of the word "addiction" itself is thought to come from the Latin term for "dedication," and prior to the 19th century the word was often used to describe behaviors in a positive light, such as being dedicated to public service or "addicted to books." But a darker view of addiction soon began to emerge.

In the 20th century the temperance movement, the development of psychiatry and the growth of Alcoholics Anonymous all shaped the disease model of addiction: loss of control over drugs and alcohol is a chronic, relapsing, lifelong disorder. As early as 1957, offshoot 12-step programs such as Gamblers Anonymous and Overeaters Anonymous applied the addiction model to problems that did not involve drugs or alcohol.

In 1980 "pathological gambling" was added to the *Diagnostic and Statistical Manual (DSM)*, the American Psychiatric Association's official categorization of mental disorders, as a condition deserving further study. In 1990 Isaac Marks, a psychiatric researcher in London, penned a widely cited editorial in the *British Journal of Addiction* describing "non-chemical" addictions, and since then the idea has received increasing attention from mainstream researchers and clinicians.

In popular culture, behavioral addictions are also getting much more recognition. Movies such as *Shame* and *Don Jon* vividly portray sex and pornography addictions. For better or for worse, sex addiction is the go-to excuse for unfaithful celebrities. Residential rehabilitation centers for Internet addiction are booming in China and even starting to appear in the U.S. Additionally, as developed countries grapple with obesity, a food-addiction model is increasingly used to explain some people's uncontrolled eating.

At the same time, however, the academic understanding of addiction is a conceptual minefield. Organized psychiatry has long shied away from even using the word "addiction." The *DSM* formerly called it "dependence," a stand-in term that emphasized the idea of addiction as a chronic, relapsing disease that is markedly different from other unhealthy drug and alcohol use.

That distinction, between "true" addiction and other harmful patterns of drug abuse, has been struck from the latest edition, the *DSM-5*, published in 2013. The update radically altered the definition of addiction, collapsing both "dependence" and milder forms of "substance abuse" into one condition, "substance use disorder," with no clear division between mild and extreme cases. That decision was based on data from more than 200,000 research participants, which showed an even continuum from the worst cases down to less severe substance-use problems.

This changing understanding of addiction makes it even more difficult to know how to define behavioral addictions. Is gambling addiction like drug addiction, or is it something else? The evidence base for most behavioral addictions is far less robust than for substance addictions, but research is beginning to fill in the gaps.

Gambling Gets Its Due

Researchers have increasingly used the tools of neuroscience to argue that behavioral addictions are brain-based disorders. For example, as recently as the early 2000s clinicians were not sure how to categorize pathological gambling. Some thought it looked more like obsessive-compulsive disorder than drug or alcohol addiction. From their perspective, pumping quarters into slot machines or repetitively washing one's hands appeared almost the same—irrational, compulsive and almost automatic.

Marc N. Potenza, a gambling researcher at Yale University, published an enlightening study in 2003. Using functional MRI, a method for assessing blood flow in the brain, his team measured the cerebral activity of people with gambling problems as they watched provocative videos in the scanner: the thrill of an unexpected windfall, the clatter of new chips, the flutter of cards.

The imaging revealed decreased activity in the ventromedial prefrontal cortex (vmPFC), an area in the middle of the frontal lobes associated with regulating impulses. People with OCD show the opposite result: they have increased vmPFC activation during obsessions, indicating excessive thoughts and preoccupations. These and subsequent imaging findings show that the brain activity of problem gamblers looks similar to that of drug and alcohol addicts.

In 2005 a group of researchers in Hamburg, Germany, used fMRI to discover further similarities between behavioral and substance addictions. They measured responses in the ventral striatum, a deep-brain structure rich in dopamine and associated with sensitivity to rewards. Drug and alcohol addicts have been shown to have both reduced activity in the ventral striatum and altered dopamine levels. This lowered activity is consistent with the idea of a reward deficiency: people with addictions have blunted responses to rewards, driving them to compensate by seeking even more gratification. Sure enough, the gamblers in this study showed less activity in the ventral striatum.

Such findings supported the formal addition of "gambling disorder" to the *DSM-5*. The only other behavioral addiction to be added was "Internet gaming disorder," but only in the appendix as a condition for further study. Debates were fierce, however, about behavioral addictions in general, and scientific commonalities between behavioral and substance addictions were the crux of the proponents' argument.

A Lot Like Drugs

Much scientific research on behavioral addictions has focused on comparing and contrasting them with substance dependence. Aside from bolstering their status as disorders, doing so can offer clues as to whether similar treatments might work, if such interventions should be covered by insurance companies, and how society should treat people who suffer from these afflictions.

There has been a plethora of fMRI studies since Potenza's influential gambling studies. His initial findings have been replicated several times, and the brain areas implicated are relatively consistent. Preliminary brain-imaging studies have found some similar results in food, sex and Internet addiction, although the results are not always consistent. Overall the findings are not as well aligned with findings from traditional substance-use disorder research.

Investigation of the neurochemistry of these disorders is also preliminary, but some researchers have found altered neurotransmitter receptor function in people with food and Internet addictions. Studies using positron-emission tomography have shown, for example, lower levels of activity in dopamine-producing regions of the ventral striatum at rest in both obese people and people with Internet addiction. PET studies of compulsive gamblers, however, have shown conflicting results. In food addiction, a growing body of evidence from rodents shows changes in neurotransmitters such as dopamine. So although there are interesting clues from neurochemistry, the jury is still out.

Another clue that behavioral addiction may be quite similar to substance addiction is the fact that some pharmaceutical treatments appear to work for both conditions. For example, naltrexone, a drug that blocks opioid receptors in the brain, has successfully treated alcohol and opioid dependence since the 1990s. More recent evidence shows that it can help with gambling addiction, and some smaller trials hint that it might ease sex addiction.

These confluences suggest that behavioral and substance addictions might have the same underlying causes—as does the fact that large population surveys show that the two types of addiction tend to occur together. Such findings are often comforting to people who wonder why they cannot overcome a repetitive behavior—framing it as a "real" addiction can mitigate shame and speed recovery. For me and other clinicians, the similarities between behavioral addictions and drug addictions help us choose and be confident in our therapeutic strategies.

Yet just as with substance addicts, people who show signs of behavioral problems often have other mental disorders that may be complicating the diagnostic picture. To give them the best treatment, sometimes it is important to look more closely at what underlies their behaviors.

Why Me?

Patients with behavioral addictions often ask me whether they are fated to be addicts—whether their battles for control are an intrinsic part of their character. We have known for many years that genetic factors explain up to 50 percent of the risk for developing addictions, including problem gambling. Just recently, genetic studies of other behavioral addictions have found similar results. A 2014 study of more than 800 Chinese twins and a 2015 study of more than 5,000 Dutch twins both found that, statistically, genetic factors explained approximately half the risk of compulsive Internet use. The exact genetic contributions, however, are too complicated to make interpretations based on an individual's genetic makeup.

Other factors can be set in motion before a person's birth, as illustrated by rodent research of food addiction. In one 2010 study, mouse mothers on a high-calorie, high-fat diet transmitted an exaggerated preference for fat to their offspring, as compared with control mice on a normal diet. This preference appeared to be passed down through epigenetic alterations that effect the expression of the genes responsible for dopamine-managing proteins in the brain.

Life experience, early exposure and a host of other environmental factors probably play a role in steering a person toward an addiction—the reality is that only a small percentage of people who engage with potentially addictive substances or behaviors end up hooked, and scientists know very little about why. Unfortunately, brain-imaging studies cannot answer that question. If you could go back in time and put Dostoyevsky in a scanner, he would almost definitely show altered activation in his brain's reward centers, but that would not necessarily tell you that gambling was his fundamental problem.

Maybe he was instead driven by existential angst, or the trauma of his Siberian exile, or even his documented case of temporal lobe epilepsy.

Explaining the mechanism is not the same as revealing the cause. From the fMRI studies of brain activation down to the intricate functions of neurotransmitters, the issue of causality is a big sticking point for the interpretation of this research. The basics are clear: the brain has circuits that respond to the feeling of pleasure and the anticipation of reward. In some vulnerable individuals, these circuits adapt in response to extreme repetitions of pleasurable activities. Yet this process speaks only to *how*, not *why*; what ultimately drives the behavior remains unexplained.

An unexpected illustration of this mystery comes from the treatment of Parkinson's disease. The illness is treated with drugs that act directly on dopamine receptors, and because the drugs disrupt the reward system, some people with Parkinson's develop compulsive behaviors. For some, eating, sex or gambling becomes addictive. Others abuse the drugs themselves, taking more than prescribed and doctor shopping for extra doses. But plenty of people do not develop any compulsive behaviors, even though they experience the same underlying influence—an introduction of powerful dopamine-acting drugs.

Reducing the anatomy of addiction to the "reward system," therefore, is too simple. Yet discussions of the reward system dominate the scientific discourse about addictions, in part because it is challenging to integrate all the other dimensions that matter—social, psychological, even philosophical concerns.

Societal Costs

When hypersexual disorder was proposed as a new diagnosis, critics in the psychiatric community expressed concern about the social and legal ramifications. Would the disorder be misused in court cases involving sex offenders? Would residential treatment centers pop up to unfairly profit from fad diagnoses, or would the disorder be used as an excuse for sexual predation?

Beyond the concrete risks, there is a popular notion that medicalizing behaviors such as compulsive sex and shopping might cast people in an undeserved sick role. There is some value, the argument goes, in preserving the opprobrium that society usually levels at philanderers and spendthrifts. Negative public perception might actually help keep some people in check, whereas a new diagnosis might inappropriately absolve them of responsibility.

If more behavioral addictions are classified as mental disorders—as they almost surely will be, with proponents continuing to muster neuroscientific evidence—there will be societal consequences. Insurance coverage, disability determinations, or the public's understanding of "mad versus bad"—the stakes are high. On the other hand, restricting the recognition of behavioral addictions could curtail identification of and treatment for people who are truly in pain. As long as a behavioral addiction is causing significant harm in a person's life, I believe it needs to be recognized.

This issue of harm, however, is sometimes missed by researchers, which leads to some odd proposals. For example, French researchers recently suggested "tango addiction." They claimed to have found that one-third of recreational dancers had symptoms of craving and that 20 percent had physical withdrawal symptoms related to the (admittedly captivating) Argentine dance. The problem, as even those researchers admit, is they could not find any good evidence of tango causing real problems in people's lives.

The gray area between clear disorders and unhealthy habits is rightfully controversial. Sometimes when people ask if they should call themselves addicts, I have to reply that I don't know. We are in the midst of clarifying and even redefining what addiction means, with our eye constantly on the end goal—to help the people who are suffering from these plights.

The Way Forward

A paradigm shift is happening in psychiatry, and many researchers now say that no mental illness fits into a neat diagnostic category. In fact, the National Institute of Mental Health is completely revamping its research program to focus less on lumping together symptoms and more on exploring the specific genetic and neurobiological elements of mental disorders. In this way, behavioral addictions are a case study in one of the trickiest problems in psychiatry: how to characterize disorders that have no definitive brain scan, no blood test and no gold standard. With time, and with more research into the underlying causes of such behaviors, we may be better able to help those who feel helpless and out of control.

One promising area of research suggests that any given type of behavioral addiction—say, Internet gaming disorder—might not be one neat disorder but rather an assortment of different underlying problems that happen to manifest the same way. This idea of subtypes was first articulated in 2000 by Alex Blaszczynski, a psychology professor who studies gambling at the University of Sydney. He and his colleague Lia Nower, a professor of social work at Rutgers University, proposed three subgroups of gambling addiction: behaviorally conditioned gamblers who get in the habit of chasing wins and losses, emotionally vulnerable gamblers who are responding to anxiety or depression, and antisocial gamblers who are dysfunctionally impulsive across the board.

Nower and Blaszczynski recently studied data from more than 500 problem gamblers, drawn from an addiction study of more than 43,000 people, and found three distinct groups that matched their model: one group with milder symptoms, one with more co-occurring psychiatric disorders, and one with severe impulsivity across many areas of life. Also, in studies of online gaming, investigators have found distinct motivations similar to Blaszczynski and Nower's model: a preoccupation with mastery (behavioral conditioning), a compensation for real-life problems, or a response to social anxiety (reactions to emotional problems). Although the evidence is still pending, some researchers believe the subgroup model can also be applied to hypersexual behavior.

The point of all these diagnostic refinements, of course, is to help the sufferers of addiction. Unfortunately, studies of treatments tailored to those subtypes have not yet shown any added benefit. Indeed, researchers in the field of substance-use disorder have argued over possible "typologies" of drug and alcohol addiction for decades, and there is still no clear consensus emerging. Perhaps the current models, which are based only on outwardly observable features of addictions, are incomplete. Diagnosis may have to go beyond the psychological features of addicts and look at their underlying genetics and neurochemistry. For example, in the substance-addiction field, researchers have recently shown that variations in genes for specific neurotransmitter receptors can predict addicts' responses to medications such as naltrexone. Considering how new this work is, the behavioral-addiction field may need time to catch up.

In the meantime, a flexible and holistic approach to treatment is best. People who consider themselves Internet addicts or sex addicts, whose problems are complicated by social anxiety or depression or other issues, need more attention to the emotional component of their behavior, as opposed to those who fit the traditional model of addiction and feel stuck in an automatic cycle of stimulus and response. Research has shown that when people have both substance-use problems and other emotional issues, we get the best results by treating all issues simultaneously.

My own approach is to aim for this inclusive mind-set. We have to assume we do not have all the answers. People cannot simply be reduced to their "hijacked" reward systems, and there is no single, unassailably correct diagnosis of or treatment for addiction. Someday a new wave of research findings may help make finer distinctions more precisely. For now, though, we do the best we can by trying to learn as much about our patients as possible.

There are no easy answers. As the examples of Dostoyevsky and Saint Augustine show us, we humans have been endeavoring for ages to understand why we get stuck in patterns of harmful behaviors and why for some the consequences from losing control are truly severe. As we begin to focus on this problem with real scientific rigor, the right question might not be "Is this real?" but rather "How can we help?"

Referenced

Do We All Have Behavioral Addictions? Allen Frances in *Huffington Post*; March 28, 2012.

A Targeted Review of the Neurobiology and Genetics of Behavioural Addictions: An Emerging Area of Research. Robert F. Leeman and Marc N. Potenza in *Canadian Journal of Psychiatry/ Revue Canadienne de Psychiatrie*, Vol. 58, No. 5, pages 260–273; May 2013.

Controversies about Hypersexual Disorder and the *DSM-5*. Rory C. Reid and Martin P. Kafka in *Current Sexual Health Reports*, Vol. 6, No. 4, pages 259–264; December 2014.

Disordered Gambling: The Evolving Concept of Behavioral Addiction. Luke Clark in *Annals of the New York Academy of Sciences*, Vol. 1327, pages 46–61; 2014.

Are We Overpathologizing Everyday Life? A Tenable Blueprint for Behavioral Addiction Research. Joel Billieux, Adriano Schimmenti, Yasser Khazaal, Pierre Maurage and Alexandre Heeren in *Journal of Behavioral Addictions*, Vol. 4, No. 3, pages 119–123. Published online May 27, 2015.

About the Author

Carl Erik Fisher is assistant professor of clinical psychiatry at Columbia University. He works in the Division of Law, Ethics, and Psychiatry and teaches in the university's Masters in Bioethics program.

What Does It Mean When We Call Addiction a Brain Disorder?

By Nora D. Volkow

As a young scientist in the 1980s, I used then-new imaging technologies to look at the brains of people with drug addictions and, for comparison, people without drug problems. As we began to track and document these unique pictures of the brain, my colleagues and I realized that these images provided the first evidence in humans that there were changes in the brains of addicted individuals that could explain the compulsive nature of their drug taking. The changes were so stark that in some cases it was even possible to identify which people suffered from addiction just from looking at their brain images.

Alan Leshner, who was the Director of the National Institute on Drug Abuse at the time, immediately understood the implications of those findings, and it helped solidify the concept of addiction as a brain disease. Over the past three decades, a scientific consensus has emerged that addiction is a chronic but treatable medical condition involving changes to circuits involved in reward, stress, and self-control; this has helped researchers identify neurobiological abnormalities that can be targeted with therapeutic intervention. It is also leading to the creation of improved ways of delivering addiction treatments in the healthcare system, and it has reduced stigma.

Informed Americans no longer view addiction as a moral failing, and more and more policymakers are recognizing that punishment is an ineffective and inappropriate tool for addressing a person's drug problems. Treatment is what is needed.

Fortunately, effective medications are available to help in the treatment of opioid use disorders. Medications cannot take the place of an individual's willpower, but they aid addicted individuals in resisting the constant challenges to their resolve; they have been shown in study after study to reduce illicit drug use and its consequences. They save lives.

Yet the medical model of addiction as a brain disorder or disease has its vocal critics. Some claim that viewing addiction this way minimizes its important social and environmental causes, as though saying addiction is a disorder of brain circuits means that social stresses like loneliness, poverty, violence, and other psychological and environmental factors do not play an important role. In fact, the dominant theoretical framework in addiction science today is the *biopsychosocial framework*, which recognizes the complex interactions between biology, behavior, and environment.

There are neurobiological substrates for everything we think, feel, and do; and the structure and function of the brain are shaped by environments and behaviors, as well as by genetics, hormones, age, and other biological factors. It is the complex interactions among these factors that underlie disorders like addiction as well as the ability to recover from them. Understanding the ways social and economic deprivation raise the risks for drug use and its consequences is central to prevention science and is a crucial part of the biopsychosocial framework; so is learning how to foster resilience through prevention interventions that foster more healthy family, school, and community environments.

Critics of the brain disorder model also sometimes argue that it places too much emphasis on reward and self-control circuits in the brain, overlooking the crucial role played by learning. They suggest that addiction is not fundamentally different from other experiences that redirect our basic motivational systems and consequently "change the brain." The example of falling in love is sometimes cited. Love does have some similarities with addiction. As discussed by Maia Szalavitz in *Unbroken Brain*, it is in the grip of love—whether romantic love or love for a child—that people may forego other healthy aims, endure hardships, break the law, or otherwise go to the ends of the earth to be with and protect the object of their affection.

Within the brain-disorder model, the neuroplasticity that underlies learning is fundamental. Our reward and self-control circuits evolved precisely to enable us to discover new, important, healthy rewards, remember them, and pursue them single-mindedly; drugs are sometimes said to "hijack" those circuits.

Metaphors illuminate complexities at the cost of concealing subtleties, but the metaphor of hijacking remains pretty apt: The highly potent drugs currently claiming so many lives, such as heroin and fentanyl, did not exist for most of our evolutionary history. They exert their effects on sensitive brain circuitry that has been fine-tuned over millions of years to reinforce behaviors that are essential for the individual's survival and the survival of the species. Because they facilitate the same learning processes as natural rewards, drugs easily trick that circuitry into thinking they are more important than natural rewards like food, sex, or parenting.

What the brain disorder model, within the larger biopsychosocial framework, captures better than other models—such as those that focus on addiction as a learned behavior—is the crucial dimension of interindividual biological variability that makes some people more susceptible than others to this hijacking. Many people try drugs but most do not start to use compulsively or develop an addiction. Studies are identifying gene variants that confer resilience or risk for addiction, as well as environmental factors in early life that affect that risk. This knowledge will enable development of precisely targeted prevention and treatment strategies, just as it is making possible the larger domain of personalized medicine.

Some critics also point out, correctly, that a significant percentage of people who do develop addictions eventually recover without medical treatment. It may take years or decades, may arise from simply "aging out" of a disorder that began during youth, or may result from any number of life changes that help a person replace drug use with other priorities. We still do not understand all the factors that make some people better able to recover than others or the neurobiological mechanisms that support recovery—these are important areas for research.

But when people recover from addiction on their own, it is often because effective treatment has not been readily available or affordable, or the individual has not sought it out; and far too many people do not recover without help, or never get the chance to recover. More than 174 people die every day from drug overdoses. To say that because some people recover from addiction unaided we should not think of it as a disease or disorder would be medically irresponsible. Wider access to medical treatment—especially medications for opioid use disorders—as well as encouraging people with substance use disorders to seek treatment are absolutely essential to prevent these still-escalating numbers of deaths, not to mention reduce the larger devastation of lives, careers, and families caused by addiction.

Addiction is indeed many things—a maladaptive response to environmental stressors, a developmental disorder, a disorder caused by dysregulation of brain circuits, and yes, a learned behavior. We will never be able to address addiction without being able to talk about and address the myriad factors that contribute to it—biological, psychological, behavioral, societal, economic, etc. But viewing it as a treatable medical problem from which people can and do recover is crucial for enabling a public-health–focused response that ensures access to effective treatments and lessens the stigma surrounding a condition that afflicts nearly 10 percent of Americans at some point in their lives.

This article was published in Scientific American's *former blog network and reflects the views of the author, not necessarily those of* Scientific American.

About the Author

Nora D. Volkow, M.D., is director of the National Institute on Drug Abuse at the National Institutes of Health.

Scientists Spot Addiction-Associated Circuit in Rats

By Simon Makin

For many people battling addictions, seeing drug paraphernalia— or even places associated with past use—can ignite cravings that make relapse more likely. Associating environmental cues with pleasurable experiences is a basic form of learning, but some researchers think such associations can "hijack" behavior, contributing to problems such as addiction and eating disorders.

Researchers led by neuroscientist Shelly Flagel of the University of Michigan have found a brain circuit that may control this hijacking; rats that exhibit a type of compulsive behavior show different brain connectivity and activity than those that do not, and manipulation of the circuit altered their behavior. These findings may help researchers understand why some individuals are more susceptible to impulse-control disorders. "This is technically a really excellent study," says neuroscientist Jeff Dalley of the University of Cambridge, who was not involved in the work.

In the study, published in September 2019 in *eLife*, researchers showed rats an inert lever shortly before delivering a tasty treat via a chute, then sorted them into groups based on their responses. All rats learned to associate the lever with the treat, but some—dubbed "goal trackers"—began to approach the food chute directly after seeing the lever, whereas inherent "sign trackers" kept compulsively returning to the lever itself.

The team suspected that two brain regions were involved: the paraventricular nucleus of the thalamus (PVT), which drives behavior, and the prelimbic cortex, which is involved in reward learning. The researchers used a technique called chemogenetics to alter neurons in the circuit connecting these regions, which let them turn on or inhibit signals from the prelimbic cortex using drugs. Activating the circuit reduced sign trackers' tendency to approach the lever but did not affect goal trackers. Deactivating it drew goal trackers to the lever (sign-tracking behavior), without affecting preexisting sign trackers. The team also found increased dopamine, a chemical messenger involved in reward processing, in the newly sign-tracking brains.

The prelimbic cortex appears to exert top-down control, whereas the PVT processes the motivational signal triggered by the cue. "Individuals seem to be wired differently regarding this balance between top-down cortical control versus bottom-up subcortical processes that are more emotional," Flagel says. Those "who are highly reactive to cues in the environment may suffer from deficits in top-down control." She suggests that cognitive-training therapies might combat such deficits in humans.

The circuit itself could also represent a new treatment target, but the exact human anatomy is unclear, Dalley notes—and addiction is more complex than a single mechanism.

Next, the researchers will try to examine these traits in people. "Once we've established the sign- and goal-tracker paradigm in humans, we can test whether these traits are predictive of psychopathology," Flagel says. "We hope this will help identify individuals who are more susceptible to certain mental illnesses or facets such as relapse."

About the Author

Simon Makin is a freelance science journalist based in the U.K. His work has appeared in New Scientist, *the* Economist, Scientific American *and* Nature, *among others. He covers the life sciences and specializes in neuroscience, psychology and mental health. Follow Makin on X (formerly Twitter) @SimonMakin.*

Recent Research Sheds New Light on Why Nicotine Is So Addictive

By Nora D. Volkow

Although our society currently finds itself focused on the tragic epidemic of opioid overdoses, there remains no better example of the deadly power of addiction than nicotine. The measure of a drug's addictiveness is not how much pleasure (or reward) it causes but how *reinforcing* it is—that is, how much it leads people to keep using it. Nicotine does not produce the kind of euphoria or impairment that many other drugs like opioids and marijuana do. People do not get high from smoking cigarettes or vaping. Yet nicotine's powerful ability to reinforce its relatively mild rewards results in 480,000 deaths annually.

There are probably several reasons why nicotine is so reinforcing, even if it is not as intensely rewarding as other drugs. Like other drugs, nicotine stimulates the release of dopamine in neurons that connect the nucleus accumbens with the prefrontal cortex, amygdala, hippocampus, and other brain regions; this dopamine signal "teaches" the brain to repeat the behavior of taking the drug. The amount of dopamine released with any given puff of a cigarette is not that great compared to other drugs, but the fact that the activity is repeated so often, and in conjunction with so many other activities, ties nicotine's rewards strongly to many behaviors that we perform on a daily basis, enhancing the pleasure and the motivation that we get from them. Smokers' brains have *learned* to smoke, and just like unlearning to ride a bike, it is incredibly hard to unlearn that simple, mildly rewarding behavior of lighting up a cigarette.

But research continues to provide new insights into the reinforcing effects of nicotine, and we now know that nicotine's insidiousness as a reinforcer goes beyond its ability to promote smoking (or vaping), extending to other non-nicotine drugs and even to non-drug rewards.

Nicotine has long been known to play a role as a "gateway" substance. Cigarette use tends to precede initiation of other drugs, and it is not just because cigarettes are more readily available. Research has shown that nicotine works to prime animals to self-administer cocaine, for example, whereas the reverse is not the case—cocaine does not act as a gateway to self-administering nicotine. Columbia University researchers Denise B. Kandel and Eric R. Kandel have identified a molecular mechanism underlying nicotine's gateway effect: Nicotine encourages expression in the reward circuit of *FOSB*, a gene that underlies the learning processes described earlier. Thus, nicotine makes it easier for other drugs to teach users' brains to repeat their use.

Even more interestingly, nicotine also seems to make other, non-drug activities more enjoyable. The movie stereotype of a cigarette accompanying other pleasurable activities is borne out by the work of Joshua L. Karelitz and Kenneth A. Perkins at the University of Pittsburgh School of Medicine, who have studied nicotine's ability to enhance the pleasure of visual stimuli (videos) and music. They have also found that nicotine reduced the speed with which smokers became bored with a visual reinforcer (known as habituation). In other words, smoking seems to both enhance and prolong the pleasure of other activities. The reinforcement-enhancing effect applies also when obtaining nicotine from e-cigarettes.

This secondary reinforcing effect may contribute to the difficulty smokers have when trying to quit. It is not simply that they crave nicotine and feel withdrawal symptoms in its absence. It is also that other activities are not as enjoyable or motivating to them in the absence of nicotine. This is valuable knowledge that may help us design new prevention strategies and smoking cessation treatments.

Tobacco remains the most deadly drug because of the huge numbers of lives lost to lung cancer and other preventable lung- and heart-related conditions caused by nicotine addiction. Even though e-cigarettes contain no tobacco, we still do not know the long-term physical health impacts of vaping, and depending on the levels of nicotine and patterns of use, those who vape nicotine may be subjecting their brains to the same alterations that make it so difficult for tobacco smokers to quit and priming them to the use of combustible tobacco.

It is crucial to understand that its entanglements with other behaviors and substances make even addiction to a relatively "mild" drug like nicotine a serious problem, and one that has the potential to harm an individual's life and health. Even if vaping nicotine is not as harmful to the lungs as smoking tobacco, its reinforcing effects may be much more pervasive than the user imagines—potentially leading not only to tobacco use but to other drug use, as well as reducing their ability to take pleasure from other activities in the absence of nicotine.

This article was published in Scientific American's *former blog network and reflects the views of the author, not necessarily those of* Scientific American.

About the Author

Nora D. Volkow, M.D., is director of the National Institute on Drug Abuse at the National Institutes of Health.

Section 2: The History of Addiction Science

Marie Nyswander Changed the Landscape of Addiction. Here's How Her Story Begins

By Katie Hafner, Carol Sutton Lewis and
the Lost Women of Science Initiative

I n 1946 Marie Nyswander, a recent medical school graduate, joined the U.S. Public Health Service looking for adventure abroad. Instead she was sent to Lexington, Ky.'s Narcotic Farm, a prison and rehabilitation facility for people with drug addiction, where therapies included milking cows and basketmaking. It was at Lexington that Nyswander encountered addiction for the first time, and what she saw there disturbed her—and reset her life's course.

CAROL SUTTON LEWIS: Before we start, just a quick note to let you know, this season of Lost Women of Science is about drugs and also, a little bit about sex. The content and the language are mainly for adults. Also, note that in the coming episodes, we'll be including a lot of archival audio from the mid-20th century, so you'll be hearing some outdated drug addiction language, as well as perspectives that don't reflect our own.

FRED WEISGAL: It is quite clear that the officials today who have been handling the narcotics problem have failed completely.

KATIE HAFNER: In the 1960s, heroin use in the United States was rising at an alarming pace. And nothing seemed to help, as this lawyer told a TV reporter in Baltimore.

FRED WEISGAL: All that they have been able to do is send people to prisons, have these people come out, and they are still drug addicts.

KATIE HAFNER: But in 1965, a team of doctors at Rockefeller University announced what sounded like a miracle: they'd found a treatment for heroin addiction that *actually worked*.

They'd been running an experiment with a small group of patients for a couple of years—and the results, they were astonishing. Their patients, all men, aged 19 to 37, had been addicted to heroin for an average of nine years. Most hadn't finished high school and had more than one arrest on their records. All had tried to quit heroin before and all had failed. But then, the doctors gave them something called methadone hydrochloride.

CAROL SUTTON LEWIS: Methadone wasn't a new drug. It was already being used to help patients detox—basically to ease the symptoms of withdrawal. The difference here was that the doctors at Rockefeller were giving doses *much* higher than those normally given—and it completely transformed the patients.

CAROL SUTTON LEWIS: One man started painting. Another one finished high school and got a scholarship to go to college. Most remarkably—the relentless cravings disappeared. They could stop thinking about heroin, stop dreaming about it at night. And it took just a day or two to start seeing the differences.

KATIE HAFNER: And yet, the Federal Bureau of Narcotics wanted all of this stopped! In fact, the bureau had been monitoring one of these Rockefeller doctors for years: Marie Nyswander. She was the psychiatrist on the team. And she'd been working on addiction for more than a decade at this point. And the men at the bureau were not fans of her work. Narcotics agents would show up at her office unannounced, and they'd come to her meetings. They thought her approach to addiction was completely wrongheaded and dangerous. But she wouldn't stop, not then, and definitely not now that she was finally seeing results. In 1965, Dr. Marie Nyswander was a legend in the making and she was set to revolutionize the treatment of addiction.

KATIE HAFNER: This is *Lost Women of Science*. I'm Katie Hafner.

CAROL SUTTON LEWIS: And I'm Carol Sutton Lewis. And this season, The Doctor and the Fix: How Marie Nyswander changed the landscape of addiction.

KATIE HAFNER: Marie Nyswander was a Freudian psychoanalyst in New York City, who owned a private practice on Park Avenue where she specialized in sex therapy. But she was a study in contrasts. When she wasn't seeing private clients on the Upper East Side she was working in a bleak tenement building in East Harlem, treating heroin addiction.

CAROL SUTTON LEWIS: Marie Nyswander was one of the most intriguing figures in 20th century medicine, and the mark she left on addiction treatment, it's indelible.

CAROL SUTTON LEWIS: So Katie, I imagine a lot of people listening to this are going to be pretty skeptical. I mean it's 2023, and clearly we have not solved the problem of heroin addiction—or any kind of opiate addiction. There's clearly more to this story.

KATIE HAFNER: Oh yes, there is. Methadone, their miracle drug, isn't a *cure* for heroin addiction. In fact, methadone is an opioid. Heroin is too, but there are differences in how they're made and how they make you feel. Heroin comes from the opium poppy, and methadone is synthetic. But they're both hitting the same receptors in the brain and body, So think about it—the idea that you would treat an opioid addiction with another opioid, it isn't just counterintuitive, it's radical—at least for the U.S. in the early 60s. And it made Marie Nyswander some very high profile enemies.

CAROL SUTTON LEWIS: But we're getting ahead of ourselves. So let's back up, all the way up to the very beginning of Marie Nyswander, in 1919.

EMILY DUFTON: She was born in Reno, Nevada to a German father and an American mother.

CAROL SUTTON LEWIS: Emily Dufton is a drug historian and writer.

EMILY DUFTON: They divorced when she was two. So she was raised almost entirely by her mother—Dorothy Bird Nyswander—who is just this really groundbreaking, amazing leader in public health, global public health especially.

CAROL SUTTON LEWIS: Dorothy instilled in Marie the importance of being of service to others and also being tough as hell. There's a great story about a time that she and her mom were camping when a grizzly bear showed up. Dorothy just clapped and told the bear to go away. And it did.

The two of them moved a few times during Marie's childhood. They lived in California, then Utah, and then New York. When Marie was a little kid, her mom taught high school during the day, and worked on her Ph.D. from UC Berkeley at night.

EMILY DUFTON: So she raised Marie to be very cultured and very literary. They'd hang out with like Margaret Mead at night, um, really interested in anthropology and very independent.

CAROL SUTTON LEWIS: And Marie, she really was an independent thinker, even when she was young. Marie was actually born Mary Elizabeth Nyswander, but she decided there were just too many Marys out there, so she changed her name. She told her mother that "Marie" had more "character."

So she was independent, but she also really followed in her mother's footsteps, and Marie decided to become a doctor. She went to Sarah Lawrence College, an artsy, progressive school just north of Manhattan, then enrolled at Cornell medical school, where she was one of just a handful of women in her class.

EMILY DUFTON: She wanted to be a surgeon, right? She didn't wanna just be a doctor. She wanted to be a surgeon. I think that speaks to her ambition. She really pushed herself to do a lot of, a lot of things that, I mean, you think about this woman in like '41, like who is pushing themselves to these lengths. Um, but she does it and it's—it's like you can't imagine her doing anything else.

CAROL SUTTON LEWIS: And at this point Marie wasn't even thinking about addiction or its treatment. It wasn't covered in any of her classes. But that all changed in 1946, when she did her medical residency with the United States Public Health Service.

EMILY DUFTON: Well, she joins the public health service actually because she wants to travel. And she kind of wants to go and have an international adventure for a while. So she joins the PHS with, with that as her goal. And where they send her instead is Kentucky. [laughs]

CAROL SUTTON LEWIS: Lexington, Kentucky, known for its rolling bluegrass hills and horses. It was also home to a massive federal drug rehabilitation facility and prison—known as "Narco" to locals. It was just outside of the city. And when Marie, this ambitious would-be surgeon, showed up there on assignment, she saw things that would completely alter her life's course.

DAVID COURTWRIGHT (1981): Testing, 1, 2, 3, 4. Testing, 1, 2, 3, 4.

MARIE NYSWANDER: I'm just sitting here comfortably.

DAVID COURTWRIGHT: 1, 2, 3, 4.

MARIE NYSWANDER: 1, 2, 3, 4.

DAVID COURTWRIGHT: This is an oral history interview with Dr. Marie Nyswander. This is June 22nd, 1981.

KATIE HAFNER: A few years before Marie died, a young historian named David Courtwright visited her at her Rockefeller office in Manhattan. She was in her early 60s then, still working, and David had come to interview her about her life and career. But, the first thing he remembers noticing was the smell.

DAVID COURTWRIGHT: I could smell nicotine. And, uh, I knew from, from what others had told me that, um, she was a smoker. And

I knew that that had led to some significant health problems, battles with cancer. And I was a little bit surprised actually, that I could still smell the, the nicotine on her.

KATIE HAFNER: Marie had smoked since she was a teenager, and despite her decades of addiction work, she hadn't managed to quit. But the other thing David noticed was it felt like Marie was sizing him up.

DAVID COURTWRIGHT: I mean, I think uh, as a trained psychoanalyst, I mean, she's obviously gonna be looking me over and judging me, and I supposed to some degree I felt that I was being judged.

KATIE HAFNER: I hear that in her voice. This cool appraising tone, and throughout the entire interview, when personal stuff comes up, she's curt. She lets the silences kinda hang there. But then, David asks about Lexington.

DAVID COURTWRIGHT (1981): And what was your initial reaction?

MARIE NYSWANDER: To Lexington, Kentucky?

DAVID COURTWRIGHT: And that, that's the moment I think when the interview really takes off. Uh, and (laughs) and there, there's some kind of role reversal, you know, where the, the psychoanalyst is venting to the patient

MARIE NYSWANDER: Well, it was a hard year. It was the hardest year of my life. Prison is a terrible thing if you're not experienced with it or if you, if you have any kind of a personality that cares about your fellow man.

DAVID COURTWRIGHT: Mm-hmm

MARIE NYSWANDER: A prison, working in a prison, will simply blow you up with rage and frustration.

KATIE HAFNER: So Carol, the way Marie describes it, I'm imagining this cold, hard prison environment right?

CAROL SUTTON LEWIS: Ugh, yes, I mean you can just imagine what a place called "Narco" looks like.

KATIE HAFNER: But you know, when we started looking into Lexington, aka "Narco," it's not exactly what we found.

NANCY CAMPBELL: It opens in 1935, and it's billed as "a new deal for the drug addict."

KATIE HAFNER: Nancy Campbell is a professor at Rensselaer Polytechnic Institute and a historian of drugs and drug policy.

NANCY CAMPBELL: That was the language that they used. They used the language of public enlightenment, the idea that drug addicts would no longer be simply considered criminals. Now, what's interesting is they were not considered criminals until 1914.

KATIE HAFNER: 1914 was the year the U.S. passed the Harrison Narcotic Act, the country's first federal anti-drug law, and soon, the prisons just started filling up. By the late 20s, a third of people in federal prisons were there for drug convictions, not to mention all the people there for alcohol offenses. This was also the time of Prohibition, after all.

NANCY CAMPBELL: At that point, the Federal Bureau of Prisons is realizing that prisons are overcrowded with people who suffer from what they consider a public health problem.

CAROL SUTTON LEWIS: But most doctors didn't exactly know what to do either. Many were getting frustrated with these patients who came to get "cured," but then went back to drugs and alcohol over and over. And it wasn't even clear if addiction was a medical problem. Was it physiological? Was it psychological? Was it a disease or a personality disorder? Or was it just a bad habit? Whatever it was, we needed a better solution.

So in 1935, the Bureau of Prisons and the Public Health Service teamed up to open a first of its kind center in Lexington—a U.S.

Narcotic Farm. Not just a prison, but a hospital too—about a third of patients came voluntarily.

ANNOUNCER: When the United States Public Health Service Hospital was established in Lexington, Kentucky, the problem of narcotic drug addiction was put under the banner of medicine. Until that time, this problem had been regarded almost solely as a correctional one.

KATIE HAFNER: And wow, this place, in this promotional film from the Health Service, you can see it. It's a sprawling art deco building, set on thousands of acres of farmland, dotted with big old trees.

ANNOUNCER: Activities include the operation of a modern dairy, the raising of hogs, and poultry, and intensive truck farming.

KATIE HAFNER: Now, there were locked corridors and bars on some windows, *but* there were also cows grazing in pastures, fresh food—everything from tomatoes to kale grown by patients on site—art therapy.

CAROL SUTTON LEWIS: What?

KATIE HAFNER: A bowling alley, Yes! (Carol laughs) and tennis courts. And everyone who stayed there—whether they came voluntarily or not—was supposed to be called a "patient" not a "prisoner."

So Lexington, it quickly became the biggest and best-known destination for people with drug addiction in the country.

CAROL SUTTON LEWIS: People would say they were going down there to get "the cure." But, Lexington really wasn't offering a cure for addiction because a cure for addiction didn't exist.

NANCY CAMPBELL: It was essentially getting people away from drugs.

CAROL SUTTON LEWIS: Nancy Campbell again.

NANCY CAMPBELL: And it was often referred to as "the geographic cure." Get them away from their old neighborhoods and their old suppliers, and also the settings, the social cues that led them to relapse.

KATIE HAFNER: A new patient first had to stop using drugs. Medical staff would ease their withdrawal often with doses of morphine tapered over the course of a couple of weeks. Then, the patient would join the general population for the rest of their treatment. Fresh country air and honest work were always a big part of it.

ANNOUNCER: Supervised outdoor recreation is desirable and necessary for the health of the patients. It promotes good fellowship and normal human relationships.

CAROL SUTTON LEWIS: There was some therapy too—individual therapy, group therapy. But, the most important kind of therapy seemed to be keeping busy—busy with work, classes, and recreation.

NANCY CAMPBELL: Which included everything from basket making to bowling, and they would graph the number of hours of recreation that patients engaged in. And, of course, the most famous form of recreation that there was at Lexington ...

CAROL SUTTON LEWIS: ... was jazz. On weekends, patients would put on big concerts and the audience would get so excited, and cheer so loudly you couldn't even hear the music. Over the years, some of the biggest names in jazz passed through Lexington—Chet Baker, Sonny Rollins.

KATIE HAFNER: And Carol, I've heard that some people actually wanted to go to Lexington just so they could practice with super famous jazz musicians.

And if you look at patient accounts of Lexington, some of the reviews were surprisingly good!

BENNY GIM: What do you think of Lexington as a whole? What's good about it and what is bad about it?

CAROL SUTTON LEWIS: In 1951, New York State held a hearing about the problem of addiction. The hearing included a few testimonies, like this one, from an 18-year-old who'd just come back from treatment at Lexington.

BOY: The convalescing period over there is very good. They've got work, all sorts. You can work as a farmer, out in a farm. You can work in a dairy, you can work inside in a garment shop.

CAROL SUTTON LEWIS: Or do carpentry or auto repair

BENNY GIM: And, uh, how about the food?

BOY: The food over there is the best.

KATIE HAFNER: It wasn't all rosy. Lexington was still a prison. People sometimes got sent there for minor drug offenses. Nancy says there were fewer riots than at other prisons, but there were some riots. Still, many people went there voluntarily for a reason.

CAROL SUTTON LEWIS: In the early 80s, David Courtwright and a couple of others started a massive oral history project all about addiction. That's how we got to hear Marie's voice earlier—as well as the voices of many patients. And for some of them, this rural escape, this pastoral temple of jazz, it seemed like it was actually working, at least for a time...

JOHN B: While I was in Lexington, uh, there was never any craving for drugs.

CAROL SUTTON LEWIS: John—last initial—B was at Lexington several times in the 50s and 60s.

JOHN B: I knew that I was an addict. But, uh, craving in the sense that people speak of cravings, uh, uh, desire, a subconscious desire for drugs, there was never that. I had never thought of it.

CAROL SUTTON LEWIS: So that's "Narco," huh?

KATIE HAFNER: I know! It's called "Narco," and then it's like this country club.

CAROL SUTTON LEWIS: Yeah. You know, it's so interesting that Marie saw it so differently.

KATIE HAFNER: So far, Lexington has sounded much better than we imagined. And I have to say, some of the things we learned really made me question whether we can trust Marie's account of the place, so we were trying to square the two versions. Here's Emily Dufton again:

EMILY DUFTON: Lexington is an extremely disturbing environment for someone who was raised like Marie Nyswander, you know?

KATIE HAFNER: Marie was raised among liberal academics, and she spent many formative years in California and New York. She even dabbled in Marxism as a teenager. A lot of the staff, like the guards, they were locals, and this was the segregated south. So, Lexington was a major culture shock for her.

Now, the doctors—the other doctors—at Lexington weren't typically locals, but it turns out, she didn't fit in that well with them either.

EMILY DUFTON: All of the other doctors are married and they have families and they're raising children here in bucolic bluegrass of Lexington. and she's like this young single woman. She's totally weird. She's a radical.

MARJORIE SENECHAL: I don't remember much about her directly. My main memories are my mother gossiping about her all the time.

KATIE HAFNER: Marjorie Senechal actually grew up at Lexington. We called her up on Zoom a couple of months ago.

MARJORIE SENECHAL: I was on the farm because my father was a doctor at the hospital there. They had built hospitals for the doctors, so there were places for people to live, and I lived there from age one to fifteen.

KATIE HAFNER: Marjorie's dad was Abraham Wikler, a big name in addiction research in those days. She told us the doctors who lived on the farm each had their own house, staffed by patients. And Carol, Marjorie said these patients would do all kinds of things for them— they'd cook, they'd garden, they'd even babysit the kids.

CAROL SUTTON LEWIS: That's a little weird to me. It's like you're supposed to be there to get better, and you're taking care of the people's kids?

KATIE HAFNER: Mm-hmm, and in fact, that is something Marie took issue with. But okay, remember that Marjorie was just a child for all this. And so she has very fond memories of running around the grounds, interacting with staff and patients alike.

KATIE HAFNER: So anyway, Marjorie met Marie when she was six or seven, and she only remembers her vaguely.

MARJORIE SENECHAL: Uh, she was pretty, and she was, she was very nice to us.

KATIE HAFNER: But she does remember what her mom said about Marie. So it turns out, Marie ruffled a lot of feathers, especially among the doctors' wives.

MARJORIE SENECHAL: Well, she did things that were out-outrageous. She wore slacks that was just, you don't do that. And she did. And she had gone to Sarah Lawrence, which showed that she was a brave intellectual with no concern for conventions and things like that. And she flew an airplane, which was pretty brave.

KATIE HAFNER: And this daring, attractive woman in her 20s was working alongside their husbands, while the women were at home, hanging out with each other.

MARJORIE SENECHAL: And so altogether, she was, she scared them, all the mothers as being too advanced. And they were jealous. I think that was really basically it.

KATIE HAFNER: And so learning all this I started wondering if Marie's own loneliness and misery were maybe coloring her impressions. Or maybe it was that she was hearing more of the conversations happening behind the scenes? Or maybe it was just that the patients had seen far worse than Lexington, and Marie was new to all this. But what Marie described to David Courtwright in their interview years later were nurses and guards who held their patients in total contempt.

DAVID COURTWRIGHT: Do you think that the—this prison mentality was related to the racial and class characteristics of these people?

MARIE NYSWANDER: No, it was against drug addicts. I, I think I could say that because we didn't have an overwhelming number, the, um, minority ethnic ratio was about the same as in, as in society.

DAVID COURTWRIGHT: Mm-hmm.

CAROL SUTTON LEWIS: So in the late 40s, most patients were white. Even though Lexington was in the segregated south, it was a federal facility and desegregated. But, there was racism. Marie said she heard nurses calling Black patients the n-word. And Marjorie saw white guards bullying a Black guard.

CAROL SUTTON LEWIS: But what would eventually get Lexington into real trouble was the research lab. As we've heard, very little was understood about how addiction worked, and how to treat it.

NANCY CAMPBELL: One of the reasons that a laboratory is set up on the grounds of the narcotic farm in Lexington, Kentucky is because the U.S. Congress says, "What we really want you to do is find a cure. We we want you to use the power of science to find a cure for drug addiction."

CAROL SUTTON LEWIS: But at Lexington, they did research on human beings, on the patients.

In one experiment, researchers put patients who'd already detoxed *back* on drugs. They "re-addicted them," and then made them go through withdrawal again. They were testing things out like how addictive various drugs were and they were looking for drugs that would help ease withdrawal symptoms. Although the research that eventually got them shut down was CIA-funded experiments with LSD in the 50s and 60s.

KATIE HAFNER: Ok, but let's wind back for a bit. The ethics around this kind of research—and research on prisoners—were definitely different then. Nancy Campbell, the historian we heard earlier, she says the director of the lab had a real commitment to informed consent, so that the subjects were all strictly volunteers who knew exactly what they were getting into.

CAROL SUTTON LEWIS: Right, but you really have to ask how voluntary participation can be when you're a patient with a powerful addiction living in a prison-hospital.

KATIE HAFNER: Right, yeah, really thorny ethical questions. Although when Marie criticized Lexington, she doesn't really talk about the research, her problem really seems to be the whole vibe of the place.

MARIE NYSWANDER: It was pretty rough, pretty rough for a little girl out of our internship.

DAVID COURTWRIGHT: Mm-hmm

MARIE NYSWANDER: Uh, and who had no idea that people like this existed.

DAVID COURTWRIGHT: Especially an idealistic one.

MARIE NYSWANDER: Well, yeah, but one who was kind of naive and had had very little experience in life.

KATIE HAFNER: And that might have been the end of any interest she might have had in addiction research, but there was something that drew her in: the patients.

EMILY DUFTON: She becomes friends with a lot of the patients who treat her very kindly. They play their jazz music for her like they give her private concerts. They make her feel human connection when she doesn't feel any other human connection in the environment.

CAROL SUTTON LEWIS: Though before we get too carried away, it wasn't all sunshine and kittens. Marie told a reporter she got mugged a few times at Lexington, and one time, a female patient roughed her up after Marie refused to give her the key to a drug cabinet.

But the jazz, the patients that seemed to be looking out for her when she was feeling alone—those memories would stay with her for decades.

EMILY DUFTON: And so naturally she, I think, becomes very interested in who these individuals are who are battling this pathology of addiction like they make a real impression on her. And that, I think, is probably the biggest jumpstart to her career in psychiatry.

CAROL SUTTON LEWIS: By the time she left Lexington, she was done with surgery. Marie Nyswander was going to be probing the mind instead.

So, Lexington is where Marie gets her start learning about addiction. But here's the thing, for the most part, what they did there, just didn't work. Remember John B, the one who said his cravings went away at Lexington? Well, he kept coming back multiple times over the 50s and 60s. At first, whenever he got released, he didn't feel any cravings. Four, five, six months would go by and he'd be fine.

JOHN B: And then, uh, all of a sudden I'll meet somebody and they'll say, uh, let's go and get a fix. And I'll go and get a fix. Like I told you, if I could afford it, I'd use drugs the rest of my life.

DAVID COURTWRIGHT: You really enjoyed the heroin?

49

JOHN B: Yeah, yeah.

KATIE HAFNER: Marie testified about Lexington at the narcotics hearing we heard earlier, and she was asked about this—how many people who went to Lexington recovered?

MARIE NYSWANDER: I, I would just say 15%. And that may be very generous, uh, very generous indeed.

CAROL SUTTON LEWIS: Oh wow, her voice sounds so different.

KATIE HAFNER: Yeah, Marie was just 32 when that hearing happened. She still had all those years ahead of her to grow jaded and world weary.....

MARIE NYSWANDER: You see, one of the things is you don't see the ones who, who have been cured. They don't come back. But when one gets a kind of feeling for it, I would say 15%. Now, I don't know how that stocks up with official figures.

KATIE HAFNER: Lexington's own figures at the time were higher, estimating that closer to 25% of the patients had been cured—though as Marie said, it's really hard to know.

So that's where we were at this point in time with addiction. These were the success rates for the best, most respected rehab program in the country.

SIDNEY TARTIKOFF: Is it your opinion that the- the best estimates of the effectiveness of cure are not particularly encouraging?

MARIE NYSWANDER: Unfortunately. Um, I don't like to admit to it because you know we always, we always feel that—uh we always have to look on the side that one must and can somewhere there is a cure. And um, but up to now, uh, with the—what we know so far or what's been done so far, it's a difficult problem, very.

SIDNEY TARTIKOFF: So that we understand this a little more clearly, doctor, this isn't some disease that responds to an antibiotic or a penicillin?

MARIE NYSWANDER: No, I wish it were.

SIDNEY TARTIKOFF: Uh, this isn't a disease which you can treat with some specific remedy?

MARIE NYSWANDER: Not that we know of now.

KATIE HAFNER: But something important was about to happen. Because right around the time Marie was at Lexington, the research lab there started experimenting with a powerful, synthetic painkiller. It had recently arrived from Germany, It had been developed by a Nazi-allied pharmaceutical company.

The Germans called it "amidone" but it would soon be better known as "methadone."

About the Authors

Katie Hafner is host and co-executive producer of Lost Women of Science. *She was a longtime reporter for the* New York Times, *where she remains a frequent contributor. Hafner is uniquely positioned to tell these stories. Not only does she bring a skilled hand to complex narratives, but she has been writing about women in STEM for more than 30 years. She is also host and executive producer of* Our Mothers Ourselves, *an interview podcast, and the author of six nonfiction books. Her first novel,* The Boys, *was published by Spiegel & Grau in July, 2023. Follow Hafner on X (formerly Twitter) @katiehafner.*

Carol Sutton Lewis is co-host and producer of Season 3 of Lost Women of Science. *An attorney who has focused on education and parenting issues for decades, she is passionate about sharing inspirational stories and helpful resources with learners of all ages. She is also the creator and host of* Ground Control Parenting with Carol Sutton Lewis, *an interview podcast about the job and the joy of raising Black and brown children. Follow Sutton Lewis on Instagram @groundcontrol-parenting and on X (formerly Twitter) @gndctrlparentg.*

The Lost Women of Science Initiative is a 501(c)(3) nonprofit with two overar-ching and interrelated missions: to tell the story of female scientists who made groundbreaking achievements in their fields–yet remain largely unknown to the general public–and to inspire girls and young women to embark on careers in STEM (science, technology, engineering and math).

These Doctors Fought the Federal Bureau of Narcotics to Treat Addiction—With Drugs

By Katie Hafner, Carol Sutton Lewis and
the Lost Women Of Science Initiative

After years of disappointing results in her quest to treat heroin addiction, Marie Nyswander was more than ready to try something new. When she met a prominent doctor at the prestigious Rockefeller Institute, now the Rockefeller University, the two embarked on an experiment that would define both of their careers and revolutionize the treatment of addiction for decades to come. But not everyone was happy about it.

KATIE HAFNER: Hey, this is the third episode in our series about Marie Nyswander. We want to remind you that there will be some adult content and some archival audio that includes pretty outdated language about drug addiction.

CAROL SUTTON LEWIS: In the early 1960s, a doctor named Vincent Dole commuted to work every day from Rye, a wealthy suburb north of New York City, to his office on Manhattan's Upper East Side.

Life had gone well for Vince up to this point. He was born to a rich family in Chicago, went to Stanford, then Harvard Medical School, and now he was working at the prestigious Rockefeller Institute, specializing in obesity and metabolism. Vincent Dole was a big name in his field.

KATIE HAFNER: But his work had grown unfulfilling. He found himself going to the same conferences, meeting the same people over and over, and then there were his patients. In 1982, he told the historian David Courtwright, he'd help them lose weight, but then-

52

VINCENT DOLE: Invariably in a short time when you kind of relax the routine, they would return to just what they had before. In other words, they were like a thermostat set at a certain weight.

KATIE HAFNER: And often, it was sheer vanity that brought them to his office.

VINCENT DOLE: Ladies would come in and announce they wanted to lose weight or move it around to different locations, and uh, I just figured that I was being kind of utilized on a cosmetic basis. It really didn't necessarily make medical sense.

KATIE HAFNER: Vince wasn't just put off by the ladies who expected him to help them slim down. He was bored. And he might have stayed in his comfortable, boring bubble if it weren't for a quirk of his daily commute. He'd get off the commuter train from Westchester at 125th Street, and then, he'd walk a few blocks through East Harlem to another train that would take him to Rockefeller. And that walk? It was eye-opening.

VINCENT DOLE: I kind of had this sense of commuting between two highly privileged oases through a truly epidemic sea of misery.

KATIE HAFNER: The epidemic was heroin addiction. As we discussed in the last episode, in the late 50s and early 1960s, East Harlem was particularly hard hit by heroin addiction, and the problem was growing.

And if he hadn't changed trains, he might have never given this much thought—maybe just a glance out the window, forgotten by the time he got to work, like thousands of other commuters. But during that walk, Vince was forced to actually see what was happening in his city.

VINCENT DOLE: And I began to realize that nobody in my community of scientists or people in Rye had any concept of that world, even though the place was right in New York. And we were living in, essentially, living in the midst of an epidemic and ignoring it.

CAROL SUTTON LEWIS: Now, addiction was far outside of Vince's specialty. But, he thought about what he did know, which was metabolism, and over time, an idea started forming. What if the desire for drugs had something in common with the desire for food? Many people had assumed that obesity was just the result of overeating, but several studies had found that there are people who gain weight without eating any more than other people, and their bodies expended less energy doing the same things. And Vince thought something about their metabolic state could also result in greater cravings for food.

What if something similar was going on here? Something about the metabolism of a person addicted to drugs that made their bodies crave drugs in a way that other people's didn't?

Now, here was a proper research puzzle, an opportunity to dive into relatively open scientific territory, an opportunity just waiting for someone to seize it. And maybe that person could be him. Maybe Vincent Dole, famed obesity expert, could even stop an epidemic. All he needed was to actually learn something about addiction.

CAROL SUTTON LEWIS: This is Lost Women of Science. I'm Carol Sutton Lewis.

KATIE HAFNER: And I'm Katie Hafner. This season, the Doctor and the Fix: how Marie Nyswander changed the landscape of addiction. And in today's episode—an unlikely breakthrough.

EMILY DUFTON: Dole was very high level.

CAROL SUTTON LEWIS: That's Emily Dufton, writer and drug historian.

EMILY DUFTON: I remember interviewing someone who said they really believed that if Dole had stayed with his work on obesity and metabolism, he would've been awarded a Nobel Prize. Like, that's how well respected this work was, so for him to drop it and be like, mm-mm, heroin addiction—that's the kind of stakes he was playing with.

CAROL SUTTON LEWIS: Vince was thinking about wading into a field where he had no experience. But even though he was very new to addiction, hadn't done any of his own research, Vince had connections. And one day he was chatting with one of those connections when an opportunity landed in his lap.

The connection was Lew Thomas. Lewis Thomas was the chairman of the New York City Health Department's Committee on Narcotics. And on that day, Vince was telling Lew about his new interest in addiction, and said, you know, isn't it a shame there isn't more good research in the field? And as Vincent tells it, that's when Lew essentially handed him the keys to the kingdom.

VINCENT DOLE: He said, well, that's a great thing. He says, I'm just gonna go off on a sabbatical to France, and I haven't seen much come out of this committee. Why don't you become the chairman of it? I said, all right, I'll do it.

CAROL SUTTON LEWIS: And that was it.

KATIE HAFNER: Okay. I just need to interrupt for one sec and say, wait a minute, are you kidding me? And maybe this is because so little was known about addiction or he was so well connected, but he gets to just become the chairman of some committee on narcotics, knowing absolutely nothing about narcotics? And yet you've got Marie Nyswander having put in all this time — I mean, she's, like, totally steeped in it. She's published an entire book on addiction.

CAROL SUTTON LEWIS: Even more to your point, this shows you how much they cared about committees on addiction if they're gonna put a guy in charge who has absolutely no background whatsoever. I mean, there was Dr. Marie Nyswander, I'm sure there were other people who were actually focused on it, but to just, to hand this guy the chairmanship because he was his bud?

KATIE HAFNER: Yeah, well it was a man's world.

CAROL SUTTON LEWIS: Yep, he gets to stroll right in and he's put in charge, but at least Vince knew enough to know that he had a lot to learn.

EMILY DUFTON: So he started reading about addiction on his own, just kind of giving himself like the survey of the available literature 'cause he had never taken a class on addiction. He went to Harvard Medical, no one talked about it. He had no instruction in it whatsoever. There are no conversations about it at Rockefeller. So he began kind of teaching himself and he came across, uh, Marie's article, and he also came across her book.

CAROL SUTTON LEWIS: In 1956, a few years before Marie published *The Power of Sexual Surrender*, she'd published a book about addiction called *The Drug Addict as a Patient*. In this book, Marie efficiently summarized everything she'd learned about addiction—the effect of drugs on the body, methods for easing withdrawal, the history of criminalization in the United States, and some of the theories of addiction from the day.

But most importantly, she argued that addiction was a sickness, not a criminal matter, and that punishing people or coercing them into treatment just didn't work. Vince liked what he read. Years later he told David Courtwright that Marie Nyswander was the only person who made any sense to him. And he saw in her, not just an expert to consult, but a potential collaborator too. So, sometime in late 1962 or early 1963, Vince gave her a call. And he reached a very tired and frustrated Marie.

MARIE NYSWANDER: By that time, I had exhausted every psychiatric and psychological treatment modality that there was. You name it, hypnosis, group therapy, moving patients around the world.

CAROL SUTTON LEWIS: Almost seven years had passed since Marie had published her book on addiction. Professionally, she was doing well. She still had her private practice on Park Avenue, and an appointment as an assistant professor at New York Medical College. But all those years of treating addiction, they'd worn her down.

EMILY DUFTON: She's been banging her head against the wall for years trying to, you know, help her patients get better and instead they're dying. And so Vincent Dole says, you know, hey, come talk to me. I've got, um, the backing of Rockefeller University with the prestige and, uh, respectability that that offers. And I've got a whole lot of money from the City of New York to try to figure out how to solve addiction. Do you wanna come help me? Do you wanna become a Rockefeller University employee and help me try to solve addiction and we've got the money to do it? And she's like, yes, I think that sounds like a really great idea. Because who wouldn't?

KATIE HAFNER: And Vince was just as thrilled to work with Marie. Vince's reaction to Marie would be echoed by others through the years. There was her charisma, for one thing, but also her straight up compassion for her patients, her determination to help them. While we've been working on this season, we've seen and heard this phrase over and over and over again: she saw her patients—from the outside to deep within.

VINCENT DOLE: She impressed me as a very intense and intelligent, uh, person who was working under absolutely hopeless disadvantages of just administratively 'cause she was all alone with a good heart and a lot of spirit, uh, trying to fight the entire establishment up and down the line.

KATIE HAFNER: And Marie clearly saw something deep in Vince. From the beginning, let's just say, they had chemistry. Though not everyone was happy about it. In particular, Marie's husband, Leonard Wallace Robinson. Carol, remember how Leonard wrote that book we talked about earlier called *The Man Who Loved Beauty* all about his beloved?

CAROL SUTTON LEWIS: Mm-hmm.

KATIE HAFNER: Yeah. Well, ha- have you read it by the way?

CAROL SUTTON LEWIS: No.

KATIE HAFNER: Oh, okay. Let me just tell you. A fictionalized Vince features heavily in it. In the book, Vincent Dole becomes "Thurman Cantwell," a New York physician who recruits "Elizabeth" aka Marie, who is also the Beauty in the book, to help him on his quest to find a treatment for alcoholism.

After "Thurman" invites "Elizabeth" to join the research team, Elizabeth is quote "glistening with excitement"—yes, you heard that right, glistening.

And clearly, Leonard is not a fan of the Vince slash Thurman character, so she's Beauty, and Thurman is Beast. And he's Beast for much of the book. Leonard's descriptions of this man, Vince slash Thurman slash Beast, they're not flattering. He describes him as slightly "cross-eyed" with a, shall we say, confusing body: "6 feet tall", "a boxer's nose", and a curiously "long head, like an ant." Little to no bedside manner with his patients. And unlike the literary Leonard, Thurman is super clumsy with words, but worst of all, Leonard writes that this man is a bore.

Again, I'll stress, this is a fictional account. And perhaps a wishful one from a husband watching his wife get a little too glistening about a whole new world that he just wasn't a part of.

CAROL SUTTON LEWIS: Mm-hmm. So back to the non-fictional account. Marie was officially hired in January 1964. And that same month, Vince brought another member onto the team—a second-year medical resident named Mary Jeanne Kreek.

MARY JEANNE KREEK: Now, you should ask me what it was like when I arrived at Rockefeller in 1964.

CAROL SUTTON LEWIS: In this oral history interview from 2017, a few years before she died, Mary Jeanne had a habit of acting as both interviewee and interviewer. And after posing this question to herself, she proceeded immediately to answer.

MARY JEANNE KREEK: Well, it was wonderful. There was a paucity of women to put it mildly. I was told by Professor Dole, whom I liked very much at the interviews, but I was told to put on a white dress.

KATIE HAFNER: A white dress.

CAROL SUTTON LEWIS: Yep, apparently, that was what women working at Rockefeller wore back then. There was a dress code. Women technicians wore white dresses, though doctors wore lab coats, which is what Mary Jeanne was, so it's not clear why she was asked to wear the dress.

MARY JEANNE KREEK: I said no, and I was told to go downstairs in Founder's to the ladies dining room where everyone had on white dresses. And I said, no and no. And as our current president, Rick Lifton, said when he first met me last September, he said, I hope you said 'blank no.' And I said, no, I didn't have the blank in there, Rick, because I'd been taught not to at that point in my life. Now I would had the blank in there, but I just said no and no.

CAROL SUTTON LEWIS: So Mary Jeanne went on wearing her regular clothes. And fortunately, it turns out women could still do research in those.

Okay, that's our research trio—Marie, Vince and Mary Jeanne. As Mary Jeanne explained it, she was the clinician on the team, meaning she did things like observing reactions and monitoring side effects.

Marie was the psychiatrist, the one who had access to patients and was most familiar with the behavior and psychology of people with addiction.

And Vince did most of the planning and research design, plotting what the experiments would look like

KATIE HAFNER: They started by going all over town, interviewing people with addictions. And pretty soon, it was clear they were about to wander way off script and try something very unorthodox, at least for the United States at the time: abandon the goal of abstinence.

MARY JEANNE KREEK: Marie and Vince and I used to have these think tanks after talking with patients and we'd hear the story—do you like heroin? Not really. You have to take more and more of it. You get high the highest 10 minutes, 20 minutes at most. Then, you're okay for about an hour or two. If you take too much, you're sleepy, nodding out. And then you go into withdrawal and you have to do this four to six times a day. It's just terrible. But I don't feel normal when I come off it. When they send me to jail and I don't have any or put in a drug-free environment, I don't feel normal. It was not that I can't get high without it. Very important difference. It's I don't feel normal without it.

CAROL SUTTON LEWIS: It started to sound like a physical condition, rather than a psychological one. The way these patients described it, addiction wasn't really about chasing the pleasure of a high. They were craving something they felt like they couldn't function without, almost like some kind of deficiency.

KATIE HAFNER: Vince had actually been thinking about this for a while, and came up with what he would later call the "metabolic theory" of addiction to explain it. The idea was this: there's something in the biochemistry of an addicted person that makes them crave drugs. Instead of some kind of personality defect, maybe a person with addiction has a "neurological susceptibility" to begin with, and after repeated drug use their neurons undergo metabolic changes—though what exactly those changes are, Vince couldn't say at the time.

It was more of a vague concept than a properly worked out theory, but it pointed them in a particular direction—because if the problem was a biochemical imbalance, then the treatment probably needed to be pharmacological. The analogy the Rockefeller team and others would come back to over and over was diabetes. A person with diabetes needs insulin. The body can't function without it, and a person with an opioid addiction might just need opioids. Indefinitely.

And from that perspective, the abstinence approach to drugs was just never going to work. But then what was the alternative?

CAROL SUTTON LEWIS: After years of trying everything and failing, Marie was very ready to try something new. And she wondered, what would happen if you just gave people drugs? Well, that was actually a question you could answer empirically.

In the early 1960s, as the Rockefeller trio set out to run their first experiments, they dared to ask a question that was controversial then and is controversial now: what's so wrong with heroin?

VINCENT DOLE: That was one of the first questions I asked, I said, gee, I don't see what's so bad about this if it's not demonstrably, uh, killing these people. And surely, taking the junk on the street is killing them, and is killing society through the crime it's generated by these high prices that they have to pay, and it's a robbery. I said, I don't see really what's all the talk's about. Let 'em have it.

CAROL SUTTON LEWIS: Yeah. I'm sure some of you are having strong reactions here. I want to be clear, heroin is definitely not good for you. Tens of thousands of people die each year from heroin and other opioid overdoses in the United States. Although fentanyl, a synthetic opioid, has dramatically overtaken heroin, heroin still kills thousands each year. It depresses your respiratory drive—and if you take too much, your breathing grows slower and shallower until you stop breathing altogether.

KATIE HAFNER: As Vince saw it, what compounded the danger was the criminalization, the lengths people were forced to go to get heroin. Add to that the unreliable quality of street drugs. Maybe, if drugs were administered in a safe and legal controlled setting—with careful dosing and without contamination—then those drugs didn't have to be so dangerous?

And this is what we call maintenance: the idea that you can keep a person with a drug addiction comfortable and able to function well— or at least better—by keeping them on drugs. Under maintenance, patients wouldn't have to deal with repeated withdrawal symptoms or the incessant cravings. They wouldn't have to break the law to get drugs. They wouldn't have to worry about what was actually in the drugs once they got them. And they could focus on other things. It was actually a well-established approach in the U.K. at the time.

As Marie tells it, her initial reaction to this idea was alarm. Once, she was meeting with a prominent medical writer named Blake Cabot. They're sitting there talking and he says to Marie, did you ever stop to think what's so wrong with giving addicts drugs?

MARIE NYSWANDER: And I almost fainted, and I almost threw 'em out of the house. And I left the room and it was just, I mean, it was like saying a prejudiced statement or something, you know. I just- I had to get hold of myself. So, I—obviously some kind of an emotional leap was made there. (Mm-hmm) And, uh, then I began picking up different information as you always do, you know, you exclude information that doesn't fit in with your idea. (Mm-hmm)

KATIE HAFNER: And Carol here, I wanna talk about this whole concept. In fact, David Courtwright wrote a paper on it called "The Prepared Mind." And that is what we see a lot in science, is it's the prepared mind that leads you to discovery.

So after years of trying and failing with these other methods, she was ready to try something new and the team of Mary Jean and Marie and Vince decided to start with the basics—find out what drugs actually do to a person. Which meant bringing people to the very straight-laced Rockefeller Institute and giving them drugs.

MARY JEANNE KREEK: And think about that. This is a pristine environment, beautiful gardens, quiet scientists, and a lovely little hospital that was created in early 1900s. And we wanted to bring in active heroin addicts, oh my goodness.

KATIE HAFNER: Not only would it raise some eyebrows, but it was questionable on legal ground, or at least it was according to the Federal Bureau of Narcotics. They believed it was illegal under the Harrison Narcotic Act of 1914, that big federal anti-drug law that restricted the sale and prescription of narcotics.

CAROL SUTTON LEWIS: And the Bureau could be scary. For three decades, it was headed by a man named Harry Anslinger, one of the most powerful men in Washington and a larger than life figure in American history. The way Marie described him, he was like a cartoon villain.

MARIE NYSWANDER: Like a movie character of a despot [laughs]. He was kind of baldish, with a very thick neck, and very ruddy complexion, and didn't smile very much.

CAROL SUTTON LEWIS: Under Anslinger, the Bureau arrested doctors for overprescribing opiates—and the Bureau decided what counted as overprescribing. Harry Anslinger finally retired in 1962, but that didn't stop him from giving this interview to a Baltimore TV station a year later.

HARRY ANSLINGER: The average addict walking the streets of the cities in this country is just like a leper. He spreads the disease. Uh, he must be taken out of circulation.

CAROL SUTTON LEWIS: "Taken out of circulation." It's chilling.

KATIE HAFNER: And this is the context that Marie and her team are operating in. Marie had been having her own skirmishes with the Bureau for quite a few years at that point. She'd caught its attention because of her earlier work with addiction patients—agents had started coming to her office and meetings uninvited. What she and her new collaborators were planning was bold, to say the least, and they did not want any trouble. Luckily, the team had Vincent Dole, who tended to get his way.

VINCENT DOLE: I asked first of all, uh, that Bronk was president of Rockefeller, whether this would cause him any problems if I got into such a politically controversial field, and I said that this problem is too hot for any doctor or institution of the country to handle so far as I know. And he said, if that's so, he said, then it's our job to do it. And he didn't ever raise any questions about any of the pressures that were on me and I suppose that he probably through his authority deflected.

KATIE HAFNER: So that was easy. And they had legal support too. Rockefeller's lawyers concluded that contrary to what the Bureau was saying, the law was actually on the doctors' side, that the Harrison Narcotic Act didn't actually prohibit them from prescribing opioids if they thought it was necessary for treatment or clinical research. And yet, for decades, the Bureau had been intimidating and arresting physicians until they tried it with the esteemed Vincent Dole.

VINCENT DOLE: It wasn't long before The Bureau of Narcotics sent an agent out who came in the most peremptory, arrogant way and hammered the table and says, you're breaking the law. And I said, well, I have been looking into that and as far as I understand, I'm not. And they said, well, you are, and if you don't stop, we'll uh, put you outta business. So I said, well, then maybe that's the proper thing to do. I said, the thing you ought to do, given the way you understand it, is to sue me.

KATIE HAFNER: It was as though he'd said a magic word—Vince completely disarmed the agent.

VINCENT DOLE: He abruptly left the discussion, and said that he would have to discuss it further with his superiors. This type of an interaction was repeated once or twice in one form or another until they became persuaded that there really was not an easy way to sort of force us out by threats.

CAROL SUTTON LEWIS: And that was that the team could get to work. They just needed research subjects. They started with two men, one, a 30-something Italian-American, and the other, a 20-something Irish-American, both addicted to heroin.

MARIE NYSWANDER: Anyway, brought in two [laughs] quiet and weak—well, not so weak—addicts, put them on narcotics, and I was allowed to put them on any narcotics I wanted, any amount. We just tried to keep them comfortable.

KATIE HAFNER: The plan was to have these patients live at Rockefeller, take various drugs, and allow the doctors to observe the effects. And as soon as the trials started, observing them became a full time job for the team. Vince and Marie and Mary Jeanne started to spend a lot of time at the clinic together, especially Marie and Vince.

In Leonard's fictional account, he describes how Marie/Elizabeth's social life began to shift. Again, I asked my husband, Bob, to do a reading. He's gotten awfully confident with his reads.

BOB AS LEONARD: Her move to bio shook up our lives considerably. She had to work harder than I'd ever seen her work. She worked very late at night now, and our social life shifted dramatically. Her friends had become mine, and vice-versa—painters, poets, teachers, mainly. But now, scientists were added.

KATIE HAFNER (off-mic): Nice, nice.

BOB: Yeah, that's pretty, that's, that's pretty good.

KATIE HAFNER: So, yes, she was drifting away from Leonard and into this new role, into this world of hard science and deeper into the world of her patients. Her old patients in Harlem had walked in and out of her life, but now her patients were research subjects in her full-time care.

MARIE NYSWANDER: I just tried to keep two patients comfortable on narcotics.

KATIE HAFNER: So what drugs would keep the patients comfortable? As Marie told David Courtwright years later, the team tried everything they could think of—morphine, dilaudid, cough medicine, even regular doses of heroin itself! But nothing was working.

MARIE NYSWANDER: The patients were not happy. They were looking at their watches and going in and out of withdrawal, comfortable for maybe an hour. Never got dressed. Never had any goals other than waiting for the next shot. The dosage went up and up, and this was not a program designed to make them high, but simply to keep them comfortable. I could not make them function. There was no way I could make them function. And so after this went on for several months and the dosage was so high, it was clear it was a failure.

KATIE HAFNER: It seemed to Marie that they'd exhausted everything, but there was one drug the team hadn't tried— methadone hydrochloride.

CAROL SUTTON LEWIS: Methadone had actually been around for a while by then. It had come to the U.S. from post-war Germany almost two decades earlier.

DAVID COURTWRIGHT: Well, it's a fascinating story. When the Americans start going through all of this technical and scientific information that they've hauled away from Germany, they discover, oh, hey, the Germans have got this new synthetic drug. And sure enough the tests quickly confirmed that it was morphine-like in its effect.

CAROL SUTTON LEWIS: It had been developed by I.G. Farben, a German company that had been so integral to the Nazi regime, it was sometimes called "the devil's chemist." I.G. Farben had used tens of thousands of slave laborers during the war, many from Auschwitz, to work in its factories. It manufactured Zyklon B—the poison used in the gas chambers.

CAROL SUTTON LEWIS: They also manufactured methadone, which the Germans called amidon. Like all opioids, it's a powerful painkiller, much more powerful than morphine, as it would turn out.

DAVID COURTWRIGHT: And the implications of this, uh, quickly became apparent, both in the medical community and to the old Federal Bureau of Narcotics.

Um, the medical community saw it as a potentially valuable synthetic opioid analgesic, and the Bureau of Narcotics saw it as that, but also as a drug that presented, um, a threat of addiction or diversion and which needed to be regulated like other narcotic drugs.

So there was a bit of legal maneuvering, but ultimately the Bureau prevailed and got it classified as a narcotic drug like morphine.

CAROL SUTTON LEWIS: At Lexington, the Narcotic Farm in Kentucky, the research center had *also* been interested in methadone, and they'd run experiments on patients. This was close to—and maybe even at the same time—that Marie was there.

DAVID COURTWRIGHT: And sure enough, it satisfied their craving. It prevented them from going into withdrawal.

CAROL SUTTON LEWIS: The problem, at least according to an early study, was that some patients seemed to like methadone a little too much. When the researchers gave it to people addicted to morphine, they heard comments like: "That is great stuff." "I wouldn't have believed it possible for a synthetic drug to be so like morphine." "Can you get it outside?" And the researchers concluded this drug was risky—it would surely be abused if it became freely available. And after that, methadone fell out of prominence.

KATIE HAFNER: So back in 1964, the Rockefeller team had been trying everything they could think of, and nothing was working. Their patients were getting high doses of opioids, but they were still irritable, distracted, and dissatisfied. And then, the doctors decide to try methadone. Since their patients had been on high doses of other opioids, they put them on equivalent high doses of methadone - presumably to avoid harsh withdrawal symptoms.

Now, when methadone was used for detox, the dose was something like 15 to 25 milligrams, maybe 40 milligrams tops. But to match the high levels of opioids they were already giving these two men, the team would have to up the methadone dose by a lot.

MARIE NYSWANDER: These were very large amounts in 90 milligrams, 80, 90, 100 milligrams. We were very scared of that amount.

KATIE HAFNER: But they went ahead with it. And the next day or the day after, there were two young men unlike anything that they had previously seen. The patients were dressed, their color was good. They seemed almost too good.

MARIE NYSWANDER: I didn't believe it. I had been around too long and seen too many miracles which turned out not to work. So I think, in a way, Mary Jeanne Kreek, who had no such past failure experiences, noticed and believed it at first.

CAROL SUTTON LEWIS: Marie was reluctant to get her hopes up. But Mary Jeanne, she could see something significant was happening. And Vince noticed it too. He had gotten in the habit of chatting with the patients every day for about two or three hours. Just casual conversations to get to know them better. And when they started taking methadone, he noticed a shift.

VINCENT DOLE: Our conversations were moving into orbits, like, uh, baseball and politics and, and more general topics that you're likely to come into rather than endlessly, endlessly recalling, uh, drug experiences.

CAROL SUTTON LEWIS: The patients seemed interested in their lives again. They were even asking to go back to school to finish their education. The Rockefeller doctors hadn't seen this with anything else they'd tried.

KATIE HAFNER: So at this point, methadone looked promising. But so far, these patients had been living full time in this controlled hospital environment. Yes, this treatment seemed to have changed the patients. But what would happen if they actually went out into the world? There was only one way to find out. But, Marie was nervous.

MARIE NYSWANDER: I didn't know how far I wanted to trust this. Uh, I could see now they said they didn't want any drugs. Okay. But now when they're out in the street, is this methadone gonna carry when they're out in the street and then they see drug addicts? They still gonna come home without a shot, they'd come back?

KATIE HAFNER: Living outside the hospital, encountering all the hardships and temptations of the city, that was the real test. And it was about to begin. The patients would still sleep at the hospital, but during the day, they'd be free to go where they pleased. And one day, off they went.

MARIE NYSWANDER: I'd sit here at night waiting for them to come back, in total terror every night, and I wouldn't go home until after they got back. And I couldn't tell them because I didn't want that pressure on them.

KATIE HAFNER: But they did come back that first day. And the second, and the day after that. Over and over, the patients came back. One time, they told Marie this story, they told her that, yeah, we saw people buying drugs across the street, but we didn't feel tempted.

With methadone, they weren't craving heroin. What were they craving instead on that day? Ice cream. Yep, instead of buying heroin, her patients told her they'd gone and bought ice cream cones.

CAROL SUTTON LEWIS: These results were astounding, but was it just a fluke? Next, the Rockefeller doctors expanded the study of methadone to six more patients, a varied group with different backgrounds, and different levels of education. And once again, same results.

MARIE NYSWANDER: They were all looking wonderful and going to school. And, and you never saw six such nice, attractive, uh, young men. And we had some narcotic agents up to meet them and talk to them. These days, we were inviting people in. So there were, I think two or three narcotic agents who came up and we were talking about narcotics, and then we introduced 'em to patients and said, well, here's some drug addicts. Would you like to talk with them? And they said, oh, these aren't addicts.

CAROL SUTTON LEWIS: It looked like Marie and her team had found a treatment plan that just might work. But had they?

About the Authors

Katie Hafner is host and co-executive producer of Lost Women of Science. *She was a longtime reporter for the* New York Times, *where she remains a frequent contributor. Hafner is uniquely positioned to tell these stories. Not only does she bring a skilled hand to complex narratives, but she has been writing about women in STEM for more than 30 years. She is also host and executive producer of* Our Mothers Ourselves, *an interview podcast, and the author of six nonfiction books. Her first novel,* The Boys, *was published by Spiegel & Grau in July, 2023. Follow Hafner on X (formerly Twitter) @katiehafner.*

Carol Sutton Lewis is co-host and producer of Season 3 of Lost Women of Science. *An attorney who has focused on education and parenting issues for decades, she is passionate about sharing inspirational stories and helpful resources with learners of all ages. She is also the creator and host of* Ground Control Parenting with Carol Sutton Lewis, *an interview podcast about the job and the joy of raising Black and brown children. Follow Sutton Lewis on Instagram @groundcontrolparenting and on X (formerly Twitter) @gndctrlparentg..*

The Lost Women of Science Initiative is a 501(c)(3) nonprofit with two overarching and interrelated missions: to tell the story of female scientists who made groundbreaking achievements in their fields–yet remain largely unknown to the general public–and to inspire girls and young women to embark on careers in STEM (science, technology, engineering and math).

Methadone Maintenance versus Synthetic Heaven: Inside the Historic Fight over Heroin Treatment

By Katie Hafner, Carol Sutton Lewis and
the Lost Women Of Science Initiative

In 1965 Marie Nyswander and her team at the Rockefeller University unveiled their findings at last: Methadone had utterly transformed their patients. By the early 1970s, these individuals were going back to school, getting jobs, and reconnecting with family and friends. One of the team's very first patients went on to college and graduated with a degree in aeronautical engineering, all while taking methadone.

But soon Nyswander's treatment started getting resistance from fellow doctors, as well as patients, who thought what she was doing was immoral.

CAROL SUTTON LEWIS: Hello, this is the fourth episode of our series about Marie Nyswander. And again, this season is full of adult content. So please listen with care.

KATIE HAFNER: In June of 1971, Jerome Jaffe was invited to the White House, but he wasn't sure why. At the time, he was 37 years old and doing well professionally. He was a doctor, running Illinois's drug abuse program. And the White House had actually tapped him in the past to do some consulting on addiction. But what this particular meeting was about—that was a total mystery to him.

So, when Jerome Jaffe arrived, he was ushered into the cabinet room with the president, along with members of his cabinet, leaders of congress, and the head of the Bureau of Narcotics.

JEROME JAFFE: And I was sitting there—I had no idea why I was sitting there, but they had—did invite me in and I thought, well, maybe that's a courtesy, because I gave them advice.

CAROL SUTTON LEWIS: We called up Jerome Jaffe at home a few months ago. And he remembered that the president started talking-

JEROME JAFFE: -about how he's gonna have a new initiative to deal with addiction. It's going to be a major initiative.

CAROL SUTTON LEWIS: Nixon said the U.S. needed to start a new agency dedicated to coordinating federal addiction treatment programs. And then Nixon looked at Jerome and said,

JEROME JAFFE: "And that man, Dr. Jaffe is going to run it." Well, that came as a shock to me, but I didn't have the—either the courage or the presence of mind to say, who told you that? And so, within about 15 minutes or so, he dr—I was taken out and presented to the White House Press Corps.

RICHARD NIXON: Want to join me here? Won't you be seated please, ladies and gentlemen. Come on, Dr. Jaffe.

KATIE HAFNER: That's Nixon at the podium in this video we found. And on his left, there's a fresh-faced Jerome Jaffe in a suit and tie.

RICHARD NIXON: America's public enemy number one in the United States is drug abuse. In order to fight and defeat this enemy it is necessary to wage a new all-out offensive.

KATIE HAFNER: To do that, the president told the room of reporters, he was creating a new agency, the Special Action Office of Drug Abuse Protection a.k.a. SAODAP—yeah, that's the best they could come up with—with Jerome Jaffe at the head.

JEROME JAFFE: I was totally unprepared. I was unprepared in terms of dress as well 'cause I didn't even know I was gonna stay over in Washington, so somebody had to buy me another shirt. And it was a—I think it was two sizes too big. You can imagine how my wife felt about hearing all of this in the newspaper.

CAROL SUTTON LEWIS: Good question.

JEROME JAFFE: Faith, could you pick up? Somebody would like to ask you some questions. Yeah, she's down there. She'll pick up the phone.

CAROL SUTTON LEWIS: After a few seconds, Faith picked up the phone downstairs.

FAITH JAFFE: It just turned our lives upside down. My husband was put in a very uncomfortable position because you don't turn around and say, Mr. President, who told you I was gonna do that?

KATIE HAFNER: Before she knew it, Faith's mild-mannered, academic husband was the country's drug czar—or at least that's what the press was calling him. Jerome was off to D.C. almost right away, scrambling to launch this new agency, SAODAP. And one of his first orders of business as head of SAODAP—a massive rollout of treatment programs across the country, delivering a drug called methadone.

KATIE HAFNER: This is Lost Women of Science. I'm Katie Hafner.

CAROL SUTTON LEWIS: And I'm Carol Sutton Lewis. And this season, the Doctor and the Fix: How Marie Nyswander changed the landscape of addiction.

HOST: Tonight from Boston, coast to coast and in color, the Advocates.

CAROL SUTTON LEWIS: In 1970, a public television program out of Boston held a debate.

HOST: And tonight the problem is drug addiction. The practical choice is this: Should your city provide methadone to heroin addicts upon their request?

CAROL SUTTON LEWIS: Quick aside, yes, many people say metha-DON, including Marie Nyswander.

Anyway, by 1970, methadone maintenance was no longer a radical experiment happening inside the walls of Rockefeller University. It was out in the world, making headlines, and people had opinions and a whole lot of questions about it. *Was* methadone maintenance really the best treatment? What about abstinence? And therapy? And therapeutic communities? Should methadone only be given as a last resort? To some people, like this doctor from Oakland who appeared on the debate that day, methadone was not a solution at all.

DEISSLER: In my opinion, it deprives the majority of human beings who get on methadone of any motivation to do anything else, and they carry on the same social and human problems with them they had before. They are just as lonely, just as alienated, just as miserable, just as sick in some way as they were before.

KATIE HAFNER: So how'd we get here? Well, let's back up. In the last episode, Marie Nyswander and the Rockefeller team were starting to see results with a handful of patients. By the winter of '65, they were confident they were onto something big.

So after that early success with the first two patients, they expanded the sample size to eight and then to a couple dozen. And then more and more and more. Note, by the way, that all of their early patients were men. Vincent Dole's rationale for this was that they couldn't risk the possibility of a woman getting pregnant during these experiments. That's a common concern with drug trials.

Methadone was exceeding all expectations. Most of the subjects stayed on methadone, and they were doing well. They were going back to school, and they were getting jobs and picking up hobbies. In fact, one of their first two patients got his high school equivalency diploma, and later went on to graduate from college with a degree in aeronautical engineering, which is incredibly impressive, and *all* of this while taking methadone.

So understandably, Vince wanted to show off their results, and soon, the Rockefeller team started hosting an array of visitors. Vincent made sure they included a lot of VIPs, like councilmen and hospital administrators. He wanted them to talk to the patients directly, to see for themselves how they were doing. Here's Marie:

MARIE: So the patients were talking, so that the public was getting to see these terrible addicts that had been in jail for years and years, suddenly on methadone, who could work, could speak, were neat, weren't robbing or stealing. So that it was a very impressive, impressive treatment plan.

KATIE HAFNER: And one day, a visitor arrived whose opinion was particularly important: Harris Isbell, the director of the Addiction Research Center at none other than the Lexington Narcotic Farm, the prison and treatment center in Kentucky where Marie had first encountered drug addiction two decades earlier. Here's Vincent:

VINCE: I thought that, uh, showing this phenomenon to him might, uh, help advance the, uh, process of research in the field.

KATIE HAFNER: So Harris went in to talk to the patients, and he spent quite a while chatting with them. They actually knew him from their time at Lexington. What would he make of them?

VINCE: And so when he came out, in this nice, gentle way, he said, well, Vincent, he says, I'm sorry to tell you, but you're wasting your time with this. He says, those are not addicts.

KATIE HAFNER: Harris couldn't believe that the men he'd just met had any substance use problems at all. Apparently, he didn't remember them from Lexington.

VINCENT DOLE: And after he left, and I went back to the ward, well naturally all these fellas were particularly interested in this interview, because they all knew him well. And when I told them this, they laughed and laughed and they said, he sure didn't tell us that when we were at Lexington.

CAROL SUTTON LEWIS: On August 23, 1965, the team published their preliminary results in *JAMA*, the prestigious *Journal of the American Medical Association*. And their paper provoked a strong reaction.

VINCENT DOLE: There was an enormous amount of skepticism because naturally this went against the dogma of the field.

CARL: That dogma being the abstinence model–where "recovery" meant being off of drugs. Having patients taking another opioid indefinitely upended that model completely.

EMILY DUFTON: It was hugely controversial. I mean, like, it was bananas.

CAROL SUTTON LEWIS: That's Emily Dufton, writer and drug historian.

EMILY DUFTON: I mean, they were, they were going against like 50 years, like since like the 1914 Harrison Narcotics Act of a singular response to opioid use, which was detoxify them and then punish them if they use it again. You know, it's just- it's don't do it, right? There's–their response was entirely law-enforcement based, and it was quite brutal. And here come Dole and Nyswander, untouchable with their money and their prestige. And they're saying like, "no, this is what we've gotta do: we have to give people an opioid every day, but it's legal and it's a medicine. It's like a vitamin, right?" And it transforms them into law-abiding, tax-paying, functioning members of society.

CAROL SUTTON LEWIS: It was an exciting time. In the summer of '65, Marie and Vincent started giving interviews, and newspapers all over the country picked up the story. In June and July, the writer Nat Hentoff, the famous jazz writer, published his effusive two-part profile of Marie in the *New Yorker*. So things were going very well for the Rockefeller team, especially for two of them. Because by this point, there was no more denying it. Vincent and Marie were in love.

KATIE HAFNER: We don't know much about just how it happened. The only person who was *really* there, was their research partner, Mary Jeanne Kreek, and when she was asked in 2017 about Vince and Marie, she sort of bristled.

INTERVIEWER: So I wanna ask you about Vince and Marie. Um, what was Vince Dole still like?

MARY JEANNE: He was a—He and Marie were not together, and a lot of people think they were married, and I joined them, and I got very upset when people say I joined them. No, Marie and I came the same month of January '64. And Ma—he was married, Marie was married. He had children. Marie was married four or five times, I'm not sure which, no children. Um, she was very quiet and not putting herself forward and yet very much putting herself forward. She was very tough and very much, um, focused on self. I'm—Not a negative comment. It was simply a true comment. And she saw Vince as more desirable than her husband.

CAROL SUTTON LEWIS: Anyway, this turn of events would obviously change the group dynamic, with Mary Jeanne increasingly feeling like a third wheel. But she was also getting pushed out professionally. First, there was the team's big paper in *JAMA*. Vince was the first author, Marie was the second, and Mary Jeanne Kreek—not an author. She's only mentioned in small print at the bottom alongside eight others who made contributions.

KATIE HAFNER: I just think that sucks. And it was only Vince and Marie's names that were showing up in the press, Marie who was getting the long flashy profile in the *New Yorker*. Because she seemed to charm reporters. An article in the *New York Daily News*, opens up with the story of a young man who was able to quit dope and get a job, thanks to methadone, then pauses to let us know that Marie Nyswander, the doctor behind this transformation, is quote an "attractive slender blonde who likes to listen to good jazz." Okay, now you tell me how that is relevant. But anyway, Marie Nyswander and Vincent Dole were two big personalities that left little room for anyone else, including their spouses.

DAVID: The, um, breakup of the Robinson marriage and her marriage to Dole was very swift. I mean, it was like, boom. Uh, it was something that was surprising to people even in their circle.

KATIE HAFNER: In August of 1965, the same month Vince and Marie published their *JAMA* paper, Marie told Leonard she was leaving him. Leonard later told David Courtwright that it all happened very fast, and he didn't see it coming. But what was he going to do? He couldn't stop her. And so in September, Marie went down to Tijuana to get a quickie divorce, which was very popular back then. And that same month, she married Vincent.

Leonard was devastated. And later, of course, he would write that novel that we can't stop reading, *The Man Who Loved Beauty*. I just—I do have to say it's an—it's an absolutely great novel, and he was a great writer. And in the book, the Marie and Vincent characters discover something called "Buteglute," a miracle drug for treating alcoholism—and a not so subtle stand-in for methadone. And as they work together Buteglute, they grow ever closer.

Leonard slash Jonathan discovers that Elizabeth slash Marie has been having an affair with the Thurman slash Vincent character. And when Leonard slash Jonathan confronts her, she flies into a rage, screaming, sobbing. But then, when she regains her composure, she tries to articulate just what made her fall in love with the Vincent slash Thurman character.

Okay, we don't need my husband Bob to read this for you. His rates are too high. I'm going to read it to you:

"'He wants to help people, Jonathan', she said very softly. 'It's his passion. Buteglute has given him his chance to be—to be—the most famous—ah—to do a good thing. And I have to help him. I have to. I have to.' She buried her face in her hands."

CAROL SUTTON LEWIS: Ooh, poor Leonard.

KATIE HAFNER: Poor Leonard. However, this scorned lover's over-the-top account gets at something important about Vince and Marie's relationship.

DAVID: I think that in addition to the excitement, uh, and the fame that came from working with Dr. Dole, Dr. Dole represented something else. He represented a return to medicine. And I think that in moving into his orbit, not just marrying him, but to repeat, moving into his orbit, uh, associating with his friends, identifying with Rockefeller, all of that, she's moving back into that- that world of proper biomedical research, and she's putting behind her this softer version of medicine with which she has become disenchanted.

CAROL SUTTON LEWIS: And methadone completely changed Marie's view of addiction. She had, through trial and error, finally ended up in a place that suited her. She scaled back her private psychoanalytic practice, and she embraced this scientific approach to addiction. It wasn't long before methadone treatment took off in New York City. As we know, things move very quickly when Vincent Dole gets involved.

EMILY DUFTON: Dole's connections to, like, the director of hospitals of New York City, allows them to start to open addiction treatment wards in places like Beth Israel and various other hospitals throughout Manhattan.

CAROL SUTTON LEWIS: Emily Dufton again.

EMILY DUFTON: And they institute these programs where people come to live in the hospital for about two weeks, and they get transitioned from street heroin to methadone, and they stabilize the dose. And then from there, they come to the clinic every day to take their methadone in the morning.

CAROL SUTTON LEWIS: And it's not just methadone they're getting. This is key. The programs were meant to help people overcome some of the problems that heroin addiction had created in their lives or that led them to heroin in the first place.

EMILY DUFTON: They're aided in finding jobs or reconnecting with family or finding an apartment. Um, you know, they're kind of just reintroduced to society while they're also, you know, on methadone and having various other medical ailments treated.

CAROL SUTTON LEWIS: But as these early methadone programs spread in New York City and beyond, they also deeply divided people. Was this really a treatment? Could you call methadone medication, or was it just substituting one drug for another? That's coming up. After the break.

LISLE BAKER: Despite what critics of the program will say, it's important to recognize there is a distinction between heroin addiction and methadone maintenance.

KATIE HAFNER: In that TV debate from 1970 we heard earlier, a lawyer named Lisle Baker took up the side for methadone maintenance. That's how the show worked: two real lawyers, arguing for and against a question in a kind of trial format. And he took pains to explain why methadone is not the same heroin. I mean, both are opioids, yes, but when a person takes heroin, the high—or what doctors call "euphoria"—comes on fast, and then, they crash.

LISLE BAKER: So he swings up and down, and up and down, and he spends almost no time in this zone of normal feeling.

KATIE HAFNER: He's pointing at a graph with a long pointing stick, even though he's right next to it and could definitely use his finger, but whatever. At the top of the graph is the green zone: feeling good or euphoric. At the bottom is the red zone, which is feeling sick. And in the middle, this is the yellow zone labeled "normal feelings." With heroin, the line moves wildly between green and red. And what about methadone?

LISLE BAKER: Now, methadone maintenance given to him in stabilizing z-doses of the glass of orange juice or tang do away with a sick feeling or drug hunger. It's medicine to solve this problem. And in large doses it can block any high or euphoria if an addict decides he wants to go ahead and shoot up some heroin.

KATIE HAFNER: So the methadone side of the graphic is all yellow. No highs. No lows. Just yellow. Just normal feelings. That's because methadone, like all opioids, attaches to opioid receptors in the brain and activates them, but it does this more *slowly* than an opioid like heroin, so there isn't the same rush of feeling, especially in people who've already developed an opioid tolerance. And while methadone is squatting on a receptor, other opioids can't attach to it. So it blocks their action. But in 1970, Lisle Baker kept the explanation simple. Methadone made people feel normal. And then he turns to his guest expert.

LISLE BAKER: I'd like to call one of the country's leading experts on this program, Dr. Jerome Jaffe to the stand.

The same Jerome Jaffe we met earlier. This was a year before he was tapped to lead Nixon's new agency. At that point, he was an associate professor at the University of Chicago and was running Illinos's drug abuse program. And Lisle asks him the question at the center of the program, the same one that had plagued maintenance from the beginning.

LISLE BAKER: Dr. Jaffe, Many of the people who are watching this program are afraid of using one drug to fight another drug. Can you help us out on that?

JAFFE: Well, I think that the problem is in the way it's expressed. Medicine has for a long time used drugs to fight problems. In this instance, we're using a drug to fight a human feeling, a compulsion to seek out heroin. Uh, we have for a long time accepted the idea of using medication to fight anxiety, to fight depression, and if we could, I think most of us would be willing to find a medicine that would be used to fight the compulsion to smoke cigarettes.

CAROL SUTTON LEWIS: Jerome Jaffe is, as always, measured, soft-spoken, and I think, fairly persuasive. But this is a debate, and he's not the only one making arguments on this day. The lawyer who'd taken up the opposing side of the debate argued that methadone should only be given as a last resort, after attempts to get off drugs have failed. And he had his own expert witness to help him make his case, a representative from the Bureau of Narcotics

WILLIAM BAILEY: At this time, I'd like to call to the stand Mr. Gene Haislip, the special assistant to the deputy Director of the Federal Bureau of Narcotics.

CAROL SUTTON LEWIS: As you'd expect, the Bureau of Narcotics rep had concerns—first, that methadone itself was being illegally sold by the people who were supposed to be taking it. This is called "diversion." And then there was the harm to the patients themselves.

GENE HAISLIP: of course, methadone, itself is a highly addicting drug.

CAROL SUTTON LEWIS: Gene Haislip argued that street heroin at the time was cut with other stuff and very diluted, so that methadone might be an even more addictive drug than the one they were trying to fight.

GENE HAISLIP: Second danger, we cut off all possibilities of an early cure in return of individuals to a drug-free existence unless we assure ourselves that far less radical and presently accepted techniques have been first used to see if this can be accomplished.

CAROL SUTTON LEWIS: And it wasn't just the Bureau of Narcotics making that argument.

WILLIAM BAILEY: Recently we went to New York City, and we interviewed 24 ex-addicts. And we asked them specifically, What do you think of the proposal in terms of this methadone maintenance program? And I'd now like you to see what they had to say.

CAROL SUTTON LEWIS: By "ex-addicts" he means people who are not currently taking drugs or on methadone maintenance, so by definition, a group that might be inclined against it.

UNNAMED SPEAKER 1: It's really just a substitute, just another dependency.

UNNAMED SPEAKER 2: I think this is a great shortcoming of a methadone maintenance program is that again they're just treating the symptom, and the public is ready to seize upon it as a panacea that is going to, you know, sort of cure all the ills of drug addiction.

CAROL SUTTON LEWIS: And this feels like what's at the heart of many people's objections to methadone. It's not solving the underlying problem. A person taking methadone, however well they're living, still has an addiction, and is still taking an opioid every day. And if they have other problems that led them to take drugs in the first place, methadone won't fix those.

And at the core of this is a philosophical disagreement that hasn't gone away. If drugs are bad for a person, shouldn't the goal be getting people *off* drugs? If addiction is the problem, then *maintenance* seems like giving up on a real cure. What about all the people who have successfully stopped using drugs through abstinence programs? Shouldn't *that* be the goal?

JUDIANNE DENSEN-GERBER: There's no reason to change a scotch drinker to cheap wine. There's no reason to change a heroin user to methadone.

CAROL SUTTON LEWIS: One of the most outspoken opponents of methadone was a contemporary of Marie's named Judianne Densen-Gerber. She was a psychiatrist and lawyer, and she'd founded Odyssey House, a drug treatment program. Unlike the Rockefeller team, Judianne's approach emphasized complete abstinence. In the early 1980s, David Courtwright sat down with her.

DAVID: Uh, I'd like to quote you from your book, *We Mainline Dreams*, again: I rarely miss an opportunity to put methadone maintenance in its proper perspective. It is my view that it is useful in only a small percentage of cases and is far from the panacea that many believe it to be. End quote. Is this still your attitude some seven years later?

JUDIANNE DENSEN-GERBER: Absolutely. Uh I've added to it only the fact that I consider certain methadone programs and methadone maintenance programs amoral- or immoral. Immoral probably.

CAROL SUTTON LEWIS: Judianne said she wasn't flat out against methadone. What she really objected to was when pregnant women were given the drug. But it's clear her objection ran even deeper.

JUDIANNE DENSEN-GERBER: I am a diabetic. I get very angry every time they talk about the replacement of methadone in the addict—

DAVID COURTWRIGHT: —being like insulin

JUDIANNE DENSEN-GERBER: Being like insulin, yeah. I become enraged. How dare they discuss a disease, which I happen to know of as a sufferer? Without the insulin, I die. Without the heroin, they do not. There is no comparison. And we diabetics should mount a very strong campaign to get us away. There should be an anti-defamation league for the diabetic every time they use that analogy.

KATIE HAFNER: Marie was unfazed by such criticism. She used the insulin analogy so many times you can't help but wonder if she did it just to goad this one very goadable peer.

Marie and those who fell in line with her thinking argued that the problem isn't fundamentally drugs themselves. What matters is how they affect people. There is no cure for addiction, and if methadone allows some people to live good, full, and by all accounts normal lives, why deny them that?

In the big 1965 *New Yorker* piece about Marie, we actually see her get into this argument. She's sitting at the storefront clinic in East Harlem, chatting with a group of patients, and she's talking about the great stuff they're doing with methadone, when one patient, a young Black man named Pete, suddenly stands up and declares that methadone is just wrong. He tells Marie they're just giving people "synthetic heaven," denying them the enjoyment of life that comes with being normal.

Marie fires back, arguing basically, well, what's normal? Patients taking methadone are working or in school. Even some narcotics agents can't tell they have addictions.

And then she says this, quote: Is a molecule of methadone more immoral than a molecule of insulin? There's that insulin analogy again, she's nothing if not incorrigible, that Marie. Then she says: "Look, if you can make it off anything, more power to you. But if you can't, don't confuse medication with immorality."

CAROL SUTTON LEWIS: Criticisms from the likes of Judianne Densen-Gerber might have rolled off Marie's back, but pushback from the people she was trying to help? That was harder. And methadone was getting a lot of pushback, especially in some Black communities.

SAMUEL ROBERTS: It's a comment, not about behavioral health, not about psychology, and what needs people have as individuals. It's about politics.

CAROL SUTTON LEWIS: Samuel Kelton Roberts, whom we'd heard in an earlier episode, is an associate professor of History and of Sociomedical Sciences at Columbia University.

SAMUEL ROBERTS: When methadone shows up, and its biggest proponents were white people who were unknown to any of the civil rights leaders in the community. Marie Nyswander had a reputation in Harlem because she had worked with Black patients. You know, she—you know, her name was pretty good there, but nobody knew Vincent Dole. Nobody knew any addiction doctors really, that were, let alone the politicians who were, you know, really promoting.

And so methadone comes out and I think, understandably, I don't think it was necessarily correct or appropriate, but I completely understand that people would say, you know, you give us bad schools, you give us no jobs, you know, you give us bad housing, we're still being brutalized by police. And as a result of all that, you know, our children are, you know, using this junk. And what do you give us? You give us more junk. Like it—politically, it is illogical if that's your perspective. And it's unfortunate that that was the context in which this happened.

CAROL SUTTON LEWIS: And it was in 1972, right as methadone clinics were opening up across the U.S., that the country was learning about Tuskegee, the infamous study from the U.S. Public Health Service where Black men with syphilis were lied to and denied treatment so that researchers could study how the disease ravaged their bodies. And yeah, that's the same Public Health Service that Marie had worked for. So when methadone starts taking off in the late 60s and early 70s, not everyone welcomes it, to put it mildly.

DAVID COURTWRIGHT: There were some Black groups who, irony of ironies, regarded this as a form of genocide. That must have made you terribly bitter.

CAROL SUTTON LEWIS: David Courtwright asked Marie about this during their interview in 1981.

MARIE NYSWANDER: No, it upset me terribly. Upset me terribly. That they could think—well, you take it personally. You can't think that about me.

DAVID: You of all people.

MARIE NYSWANDER: [Laughs] But I really felt very bad, because here was poor Harlem, which was just being decimated by drug addiction, destroyed by drug addiction. Perhaps one out of every fifteen, twenty men were drug addicts up there. For some of their medical profession and leaders to turn against the only possible salvation they had—meanwhile, we have Black people going back to school and doing so well, uh, that was a heartbreaker.

CAROL SUTTON LEWIS: "The only possible salvation they had." There's a whiff of that famous Marie savior complex again, along with a good dose of condescension.

KATIE HAFNER: But in the early 70s, as we heard earlier, methadone was getting a lot of support at the highest level of government with Nixon's war on drugs. And from the start, methadone was one of the biggest weapons in his arsenal. This wasn't necessarily because he cared deeply about people with addiction. Heroin addiction was driving crime. Voters didn't like that. And it was hurting the war effort. In 1971, two congressmen visited Vietnam and came back with a shocking finding: 10 to 15 percent of soldiers were addicted to heroin, and they were bringing their addictions back with them. If methadone could help with these problems, well, it was a means to an end. And so that's why Nixon brought on the very pro-methadone Jerome Jaffe.

DAVID COURTWRIGHT: That- that was an interesting time. Not only does President Nixon declare a war on drugs, but it's a different kind of drug war. There's a lot of emphasis on treatment as—as well as simply law enforcement.

KATIE HAFNER: There has always been this tension in the country's approach to drug addiction—between law enforcement as embodied by federal narcotics agencies versus treatment, as embodied by offices like Nixon's SAODAP. And as head of SAODAP, Jerome Jaffe moved quickly. When he first arrived in Washington, he had no budget and no staff, but he soon managed to get the agency up and running, and it wasn't long before he was rolling out methadone maintenance programs across the country. In 1971, there were about 9000 patients on methadone maintenance. By 1973, two years later, that number had grown to 73,000. Methadone wasn't the only treatment SAODAP was rolling out, but it was a big and highly visible one, and soon, critics were calling Jaffe "the methadone king."

DAVID: And so that's why the honeymoon ends because with growth comes problems. There's the so-called NIMBY phenomenon, the not in my backyard phenomenon, uh, where people in the neighborhood don't want a methadone clinic. So you've got a local opposition.

CAROL SUTTON LEWIS: In neighborhoods with methadone clinics, people started seeing long lines of patients waiting to get their daily dose. And a lot of residents did not want them there. Locals would tell newspapers they were worried about drug users coming into their neighborhoods, coming near their children. And federal regulators were worried about these clinics too.

DAVID: Not every methadone program was a clean program. There was diversion of methadone into the black market.

CAROL SUTTON LEWIS: Methadone is still an opioid, and even though it wasn't as fast-acting and doesn't produce a high like some other opioids, it still had street appeal. And as more clinics were established, so-called "pill mills" started popping up.

DAVID: People would go to a privately run methadone clinic and the doctor would say, how many pills do you want? And you would be charged on the basis of, you know, the size of the prescription for, um, methadone tablets that he would write for you. And, uh, it's obvious that not all of those were being consumed by the individuals. They would leave, and they would sell those pills on the street for cash because word got around fast that if you were undergoing withdrawal and you couldn't get a, uh, an injection of heroin, if you could get a hold of some diverted me, that would tide you over.

CAROL SUTTON LEWIS: This development seemed to confirm what the Federal Bureau of Narcotics had been worried about in the first place.

JAFFE: It was an odd situation with methadone, which if left to its own devices, which essentially allowed people to do whatever they wanted, uh, would result in overdoses, uh, and deaths. They wouldn't be overdoses among the addicts themselves, but there would be some. There would also be deaths of non-drug users. You know, you would, your medicine in the refrigerator and an eight year old would take it. Uh, and these were dramatized by the media.

CAROL SUTTON LEWIS: The Bureau of Narcotics seized on these stories, teaming up with the FDA to more strictly regulate methadone. The FDA announced that methadone was an investigational drug in 1970 which meant it could more closely control how these clinics operated.

KATIE HAFNER: And not long after, federal law enforcement finally got the control they wanted. By that time Jerome Jaffe was no longer in charge, and the Bureau of Narcotics had been superseded by the Drug Enforcement Agency.

JAFFE: The Drug Enforcement Agency came to Congress insisting that there was so much overdoseage that Congress ought to give them co-authority over methadone programs. They were given authority to look to the security of methadone at methadone clinics. But often, uh, at least in my experience, they pushed the limits of what they were authorized to do.

CAROL SUTTON LEWIS: By the time Marie sat down with David Courtwright in 1981, methadone was a highly bureaucratized system, bogged down by intense regulations. And Marie was not happy. Why couldn't patients go to a doctor, get a prescription like they would for any other medication? If a patient is doing well, why can't they get a one month supply? Why do they have to line up outside a clinic each morning?

MARIE: Many of my patients here get four months or four weeks medication. They travel, no problem, never been a problem for 17 years. So I do think that is the, the future. it is absurd to keep them—It's part of also keeping them isolated or the finger pointed on them, reminding them, uh, of what unreliable people they are that they have to be segregated to methadone clinic.

CAROL SUTTON LEWIS: The thing that Marie had fought so hard against, that stigma, persisted. When David spoke with patients, many of them said that methadone had helped keep them stable, but still, they felt people were judging them.

JOHN B: Nobody in my family knows anything about this type of thing.

CAROL SUTTON LEWIS: John B, who we heard from in the first episode, he was in and out of Lexington for years, and couldn't find a way out of his heroin addiction. Methadone finally allowed him that, but—

JOHN B: I go to visit my family, uh, yearly and, uh, nobody knows that I am on a methadone program and I have to take medication with me and, uh, the people at the program, uh, suggested that I go to one of the programs in my town and get some methadone. I wouldn't dare do that. My family's too well known in the town.

CAROL SUTTON LEWIS: Another patient, Stella, found methadone helpful too, but professionally, it was causing a problem.

STELLA: I haven't taken any kind of drugs since I'm on the program. In fact, I got a job in the telephone company, and after two months, I had to go for an examination and they found out that I had, uh, methadone in my urine, and they fired me.

INTERVIEWER: Did you get another job while you were on methadone?

STELLA: I tried. Being that I can type, I tried, uh, I went to the state building on 125th Street and I told them that I would like to brush up on my typing. But at the same time, I told them I was on the methadone program, and they said they wouldn't take me. They don't take people who are on meth programs.

CAROL SUTTON LEWIS: As Marie saw it, the tight regulation of methadone was feeding this problem. In their conversation, David asked Marie what kind of narcotics policy she'd like to see in the U.S.

MARIE: Well, hopefully, research would continue to find a better drug than methadone, hopefully a cure, but it's a chronic disease, and we don't do very well with any cures in chronic diseases. So that the research would continue to go on, and that the clinics would go on with a kind of understanding that they had when they first opened. We—we didn't have any federal rules they told us that mandated treatment or urine tests or anything else. The doctor did what- what seemed indicated, and patients could take two or three weeks right at the beginning if they were working and needed it. No problem.

DAVID: You're starting to sound like a Republican.

MARIE: [Laughter] Like a Republican.

DAVID: Complaining about federal regulations.

KATIE HAFNER: All joking aside, Marie was frustrated. She was a person with strong opinions, and this was something she'd been working on for years and years and years, an intractable problem, and she had found methadone, and methadone was her baby. It was her game-changing treatment, her legacy, the quote "only salvation" as she saw it. And now, it was finally out there in the world, but not the way she wanted.

About the Authors

Katie Hafner is host and co-executive producer of Lost Women of Science. *She was a longtime reporter for the* New York Times, *where she remains a frequent contributor. Hafner is uniquely positioned to tell these stories. Not only does she bring a skilled hand to complex narratives, but she has been writing about women in STEM for more than 30 years. She is also host and executive producer of* Our Mothers Ourselves, *an interview podcast, and the author of six nonfiction books. Her first novel,* The Boys, *was published by Spiegel & Grau in July, 2023. Follow Hafner on X (formerly Twitter) @katiehafner.*

Carol Sutton Lewis is co-host and producer of Season 3 of Lost Women of Science. *An attorney who has focused on education and parenting issues for decades, she is passionate about sharing inspirational stories and helpful resources with learners of all ages. She is also the creator and host of* Ground Control Parenting with Carol Sutton Lewis, *an interview podcast about the job and the joy of raising Black and brown children. Follow Sutton Lewis on Instagram @groundcontrol-parenting and on X (formerly Twitter) @gndctrlparentg.*

The Lost Women of Science Initiative is a 501(c)(3) nonprofit with two overarching and interrelated missions: to tell the story of female scientists who made groundbreaking achievements in their fields–yet remain largely unknown to the general public–and to inspire girls and young women to embark on careers in STEM (science, technology, engineering and math).

Section 3: Opioid Addiction

Against Medical Advice: Another Deadly Consequence of Our Opioid Epidemic

By Zoe Adams

A t 3 a.m., a high-pitched beep rang on my pager from a patient's nurse. The page read: "Please come to bedside ASAP. Patient agitated and threatening to leave AMA. Security on their way."

Like many medical trainees, I have received countless pages like this one. Fred (not his real name), a patient in his 60s with a history of opioid use disorder, was trying to leave "against medical advice," or AMA. He was admitted to the hospital for opioid withdrawal and to treat pneumonia, which required IV antibiotics.

I ran up three flights of stairs. I hadn't written down Fred's room number, but I could immediately tell which room was his: three suited security guards, two nurses and the crackling of walkie talkies were giveaways.

The next thing I knew security guards were strip searching Fred, going through his belongings and throwing them into plastic bags that brandished the hospital's logo. His nurse demanded he take off his socks and shirt, and empty his wallet. He grew angry, and as he emptied his wallet, dollar bills fell from his hospital bed to the floor. He threw his socks across the room.

"I found him secretly using a vape pen," the nurse said. "We needed to search his belongings for any other contraband. It's a safety concern."

A vape pen? Not exactly contraband.

The security guards and I tried to deescalate, but Fred could no longer withstand being punished. So he decided to leave. The response to his vaping—a minor infraction that posed no threat to staff—was inappropriate, humiliating and unjust. His medical team failed to provide the treatment he deserved. And it all could have been avoided.

93

Compared with other patient populations, people who struggle with addiction are at the highest risk of leaving the hospital prematurely. A recent study in the *Journal of the American Medical Association* revealed that patients with opioid use disorder are particularly susceptible to leaving the hospital early.

From 2016 to 2020, the annual rate for patients leaving "against medical advice" after they are admitted to hospitals with opioid use disorder from over 30 states increased from approximately 9 to 17 percent. In contrast, the rate for all nonopioid admissions remained around 1 percent during that time period. These discharges can be deadly and expensive. They are associated with twice the odds of all-cause death and hospital readmission within 30 days.

When people with addiction explain why they leave the hospital, they cite untreated withdrawal, pain, discrimination about their addiction, and hospital restrictions, such as not being able to leave the hospital floor for a walk or smoke break.

Stigma against patients with addiction is rampant among the medical community—from physicians and nurse practitioners to registered nurses and social workers. At the residency level, most physicians do not receive adequate training in addiction medicine, such as how to treat opioid withdrawal or co-occurring pain. This leaves these patients at risk of poor care and serious medical complications.

The phrase *against medical advice* is dripping with accusation and blame. When a patient leaves prematurely, providers frame it as the patient's fault. But hospital care teams have a tremendous role to play as to whether someone decides to leave the hospital. And when someone does, it reflects a broader failure of the treatment team.

Hospital policies change constantly to improve patient outcomes. Hospital administrators should see premature discharges among people with substance use disorder as an urgent problem. Preventing these discharges is part of responding to the nation's addiction and overdose crisis, which kills more than 100,000 people a year in the U.S. One in nine hospitalizations across the U.S. are for adults with substance use disorder.

We need to take patients' complaints seriously. Hospitals could have designated vaping zones for patients. Or hospital administrators could hire recovery coaches to accompany patients on smoke breaks. Social workers could respond to pages about agitated patients instead of armed security guards. Providers could also begin to normalize that patients with addiction might have their substance of choice on them in the hospital. While use should be prohibited, possession of a substance should not lead to punitive action.

To be sure, it is essential that health care providers continue to prioritize the safety of patients and medical staff—especially nurses—who are on the front lines of patient care. It is not acceptable for patients to abuse staff, verbally or physically. However, a patient threatening physical abuse and a patient using a vape pen must warrant different responses. Stigma against people who use drugs certainly influences a provider's perceived level of "safety."

After Fred left, I felt ashamed. He came to the hospital in withdrawal seeking medication for opioid addiction and struggling to breathe from pneumonia. The system failed him on both fronts. Health care providers and hospital administrators must do better so that patients with addiction continue to seek care at our nation's hospitals. Their lives—and dignity—depend on it.

This is an opinion and analysis article, and the views expressed by the author or authors are not necessarily those of Scientific American.

About the Author

Zoe Adams is a Public Voices Fellow of The OpEd Project and a resident physician at Massachusetts General Hospital. Her writing and research have been published in the Washington Post, Guernica *magazine and the* Journal of the American Medical Association.

We're Overlooking a Major Culprit in the Opioid Crisis

By Maia Szalavitz

J ournalists have largely presented the overdose crisis as a story of three interconnected and perhaps inevitable waves. First, drug companies, led by Purdue Pharma, maker of the notorious OxyContin, convinced gullible doctors to prescribe unneeded opioids. This led to hundreds of thousands of new addictions in the 1990s and 2000s. Observational research suggested that opioid prescribing was linked with increased disability and decreased productivity.

And overdose deaths began to rise.

The second wave in this narrative begins around 2011, when states cracked down on "pain clinics" that were really pill mills, offering doses for dollars. Prescriptions became scarce, prices rose and people who were addicted began to turn to heroin, which was cheaper and now had a big enough pool of customers to attract cartels to places that they'd never served before. Again, overdose deaths increased.

Finally, the third wave was initiated by dealers about four years later. Seeing a chance to make even more money, they began to cut heroin with illicitly manufactured fentanyl and various other synthetic opioids, which are both cheaper to make and more potent. Once again, addiction worsened. Nearly 100,000 people are thought to have died from overdose in 2020, the deadliest toll from overdose in American history.

This is the story being told in ongoing litigation against Purdue and other manufacturers and distributors of opioids. It's being told now in West Virginia in a case against the three major distributors to pharmacies—a case seen as a landmark for thousands of similar cases.

But while the media has focused on the harm done by Big Pharma, it has largely ignored the greater damage done by policies intended to solve the problem.

96

Advocates led mainly by a group called Physicians for Responsible Opioid Prescribing made the case to policy makers and politicians that since overprescribing caused the epidemic, reducing medical use would solve the problem. And they did succeed in significantly shrinking the medical supply: since 2011, opioid prescribing has been cut by more than 60 percent.

Unfortunately, however, as medical use declined, the total number of overdose deaths more than *doubled* between 2011 and 2020. Indeed, even before the pandemic, more overdose deaths had occurred since prescribing began to fall than took place while medical opioid use was soaring.

The fact that cutting the medical supply could potentially make matters worse didn't seem to factor in to the calculations of those who supported this approach. But this outcome was, in fact, completely predictable—so much so that the phenomenon has an academic name, "the iron law of prohibition."

Coined by activist Richard Cowan in 1986, the phrase refers to the effects of reducing drug supplies while not acting significantly to manage demand. Almost always, it results in the rise of a more harmful drug because of a simple physical fact: hiding smaller things is easier than hiding bigger ones. So, because illegal drugs need to be concealed, prohibition favors more potent and therefore more potentially deadly substances.

This was seen even during alcohol prohibition, when hard liquor was preferred for sale over lower-alcohol wine and beer. Whisky is roughly eight times more potent than beer—so, it's much easier to stash. Hence, we refer to alcohol smugglers as bootleggers, because they could hide flasks in their boots—not, say, "barrel hiders."

During today's overdose crisis, the iron law meant that when people with addiction lost access to pharmaceuticals like oxycodone (the active drug in OxyContin), they created a massive demand for street opioids. Historically, the most common of these has been heroin, but aided by the internet, dealers soon found a cheaper and more potent substitute: fentanyl and similar synthetics, which can be hundreds to thousands of times stronger.

It's not clear what the thinking was here: did policy makers believe that simply taking away drugs cures addiction? Or pain? Regardless, drug dealers were far more nimble than the government, often trolling for customers outside the offices of shuttered pill mills.

There's also another reason that this supply-side policy was predictably dangerous.

That is, legitimate pharmaceuticals are required to be of a standard dosage and purity, which means that people know how much they are taking and whether it's more or less than usual. Street drugs, by contrast, are unregulated. It's difficult to be sure what's in that mystery pill or powder, let alone what the appropriate dose should be.

Though advocates of cutting the medical supply argued that prescription opioids are just "heroin pills," and should be seen as similarly risky, this misses a critical distinction. If pharmaceutical and street versions of drugs are in fact equally safe, there'd be no need for regulators like the FDA. Sure, people can misuse both, but with pharmaceuticals, at least they have the option of dosing more safely. This fact makes using street drugs more deadly.

Moreover, it's not like policy makers couldn't have acted on the demand side. We have two medications— buprenorphine (brand name: Suboxone) and methadone— that are proven to cut the overdose death rate by 50 percent or more. We could have immediately made them available to patients with addiction when shutting down rogue doctors.

And this would have been a far easier task than trying to track down and treat people who use illegal drugs after their suppliers were taken down. Unlike street dealers, doctors must have a list of the real names of the patients to whom they prescribe: pharmacies require government ID like a driver's license in order to dispense controlled substances.

If the goal of reducing prescribing were actually to help addicted people and improve pain care, these patients could have been contacted and given immediate access to appropriate treatment for their medical conditions when they lost their doctors. This would have left far fewer customers for dealers.

Instead, however, supply was simply cut and, in some cases, thousands of people were left to suffer withdrawal at the same time. As the crackdown progressed, even doctors who see their patients as benefitting from opioids began either to reduce doses or stop prescribing entirely for fear of being targeted by police and medical boards. Now, half of all general practitioners will not even accept new patients who have lost their doctors and want to continue opioid treatment.

Health departments can see the problem coming when pain clinics shut down. These days, some even issue alerts about a likely rise in overdose calls. But if the goal here is to save lives, why are these patients left at risk without even being offered help first? (The only published example I've found of law enforcement trying to aid patients in this situation was during a huge 2019 raid; why is this a rarity, rather than the rule?).

Further, none of this addresses the increased disability and suicidal thoughts that can occur when pain patients are deprived of the only treatment that they have found to bring relief. Though opioids were certainly overused, some intractable pain patients do benefit, and only lip service has been given to helping them. The result is that hundreds of thousands of people have simply had their opioid medications reduced or eliminated, regardless of whether this improved or destroyed their lives.

And research suggests that these cuts often haven't helped people with pain. One study of millions of medical records, which compared the timing of state opioid regulations and reductions and could therefore suggest causality, found that opioid *reductions* actually led directly to increased disability, decreased productivity, rising medical costs and more pain. Another study found that among veterans who had their opioids stopped involuntarily, 9 percent became suicidal and 2 percent actually tried to take their own lives. Even worse, other research shows that rather than minimizing overdose risk, cutting access to medical opioids nearly triples the odds of overdose death among people in pain.

Journalists continue to echo the three-wave story that places the blame overwhelmingly on pharma. But the second two phases didn't just happen: they were driven by policy choices.

And few have called for accountability for those who initiated the medical supply crackdown that drove the rise of fentanyl.

So, where is the reckoning for policy makers, from the DEA to the CDC to Congress and state legislatures, who closed pill mills and wrote laws, guidelines and regulations to decrease prescribing, while making no significant effort to immediately treat any of the abandoned patients, whether they were addicted or in pain or both?

Why are we still spending hundreds of millions of dollars on policing and cutting the medical supply, while more than 80 percent of people with opioid use disorder still don't have access to effective treatment and while the vast majority of overdose deaths are now caused by street fentanyl and its chemical cousins, not prescriptions? Why do we ignore the fact that most opioid addictions start when people take drugs that are not prescribed to them?

Of course, there are potential negative effects from many kinds of policies, and lawsuits really aren't the best way to hold policy makers accountable. Moreover, unlike in Purdue Pharma's case, many of these efforts were made in good faith.

But if we actually want to use the money obtained by suing drug makers effectively, we can't ignore the fact that the supply-side "cure" that we've enacted so far has actually worsened the disease. It's understandable to want to punish drug makers for the genuine harm they have caused. To do better, however, we need to base policy on evidence, not emotion.

This is an opinion and analysis article.

About the Author

Maia Szalavitz is the author of, most recently, Undoing Drugs: The Untold Story of Harm Reduction and the Future of Addiction. *She is a contributing opinion writer for the* New York Times *and author or co-author of seven other books.*

How to Break the Bonds of Opioids

By Claudia Wallis

At 6 feet, 3 inches tall, Brett Muccino is a big man with a powerful frame, so he finds it hard to imagine how he could have flown through the narrow windshield of his old Ford Ranger. "It was a little, tiny thing," he recalls. The devastating 1986 car crash crunched vertebrae in his neck and lower back. It also launched a 34-year battle with chronic pain and a love-hate relationship with the opioids he relied on to manage it.

On a sunny fall day Muccino was decked out in a hat and jacket emblazoned with the words "Vietnam Veteran" while visiting the West Haven VA Medical Center in Connecticut. He moved haltingly through the long corridors of polished linoleum, slightly bent over a walker. A bad back is not the only source of misery for this retired nursing home operations director. Diabetic nerve damage—the VA attributes his diabetes to wartime Agent Orange exposure—has rendered his feet and his hands painful, tingly and unreliable. He also suffers from chronic infections around an artificial knee.

Muccino, now 68, had come to West Haven's Opioid Reassessment Clinic after a long and perilous journey that included seven spinal surgeries and escalating doses of opioids when the operations, and physical therapy, failed to bring relief. In the 1990s doctors switched him from short-acting Percocet to 40 milligrams a day of a hot new drug: long-acting OxyContin. Within a few months he needed twice the dose, but "at least it allowed me to work," he says. No one told him it was addictive. He found out when a surgeon cut him off shortly before a back procedure. "It was cold turkey with no discussion of what I was going to go through," he recalls. Within 48 hours he was in an emergency room wracked by the agony of withdrawal—screaming in pain, shaking and unable to hold down food. Back on opioids, he began supplementing his prescription by buying drugs on the street and later from an unscrupulous doctor, taking upward of 320 milligrams of Oxy a day. He would try to get clean periodically, but pain always brought him back.

By the summer of 2016 Muccino was sick to death of the whole vicious cycle. After his final back surgery brought him some relief, he told his doctors, "I want off of everything." His timing was good: a few years earlier the VA had opened this specialized clinic less than an hour from his home. Its team helped him learn a variety of pain-management techniques and gave him a medication that both reduces pain and controls withdrawal symptoms. Thus began a slow, many-months taper of Oxy that ended up at his goal: zero.

Muccino's struggles are common, but the help he has received is rare. As U.S. deaths from both legal and illegal opioids exploded from 9,489 in 2001 to 47,600 in 2017, the country began a widespread crackdown on the prescription painkillers. Health authorities, insurance companies, medical groups and even pharmacies began cutting off patients and sharply limiting dosages. The restrictions have caused anguish among the seven million to 10 million people who take these medications for chronic pain that stems from conditions ranging from fibromyalgia to spinal cord injuries to tissue damage left by war wounds or surgery. Even though illegal drugs (especially illicit fentanyl) cause the majority of overdoses, policy makers were alarmed that more than a third of opioid deaths involved prescription pills. In 2016 the Centers for Disease Control and Prevention issued a guideline, reminding doctors that the drugs should be used only as a last resort for chronic pain. It cautioned against prescribing daily doses above 50-milligram morphine equivalents (MMEs are a way to equate the doses of various opioids). States also jumped into action. At least 36 issued policies or guidelines that in some way limited the amount of opioids that doctors could prescribe. In addition, many doctors misconstrued the CDC guideline as a hard limit on dosage—even for long-term users. By 2017 almost 70 percent of family medicine physicians had cut back on prescribing the drugs, and nearly 10 percent stopped offering them altogether, according to a *Boston Globe* survey.

Abruptly cutting off patients, however, is a dangerous practice that can cause their pain to spike and lead them to turn to street drugs or suicide, experts warn. "It creates intense destabilization, both medically and psychologically," says pain psychologist Beth Darnall of the Stanford University School of Medicine. She was among 92 experts and advocates who wrote an open letter in September 2018 to the federal Pain Management Task Force warning of "an alarming increase in reports of patient suffering and suicides." Last April both the CDC and the Food and Drug Administration took action to warn doctors about these risks.

There is no question that cold-turkey cutoffs are bad, but sadly, there is a lot less clarity about how best to reduce opioid dependence among chronic pain patients. There never was much science to justify using these powerful drugs for months and years at a time and precious little to show how to reverse course. Fortunately, research, fueled by an influx of federal dollars, is beginning to point the way. Among the early findings: tapering long-term users appears to work best when done very slowly, with close individualized attention and instruction in alternative ways to handle pain—much the way Muccino has been helped. Surprisingly, some studies suggest that many patients wind up feeling better on lower doses or none at all, as side effects such as lethargy, mental fog and extreme constipation fade away. A new guide to dose reduction, issued last October by the U.S. Department of Health and Human Services (HHS), endorses these go-slow, collaborative, "patient-centered" techniques.

Many key questions remain the subject of ongoing studies, including such basic issues as when these drugs remain appropriate for chronic pain and at what doses, who truly needs to be tapered from opioids, and how best to go about it when patients are reluctant and fearful. "The pain research question that probably has the biggest impact on society right now is: What is the long-term safety and effectiveness of opioids?" says Sean Mackey, chief of the division of pain medicine at Stanford. "The reality is, we don't know." But slowly and surely, answers are arriving to safely unwind the great American love affair with opioids.

The Opioid Attraction

The idea that opioids are an appropriate choice for pain that is chronic—lasting more than three months—took off in the mid-1990s. It was a period when the medical community had begun to take pain more seriously in general, labeling it "the fifth vital sign" (after blood pressure, pulse, respiratory rate and temperature). It was also when OxyContin, an extended-release version of the opioid oxycodone, was introduced with much fanfare, along with some seriously misleading claims about its long-term safety and nonaddictive nature—claims that later became the subject of multimillion-dollar lawsuits. Prior to that, natural opiates such as morphine and synthetic opioids such as oxycodone were mainly used for acute short-term pain, cancer and palliative care. According to a CDC analysis, prescriptions for opioids quadrupled between 1999 and 2010.

The drugs were seen as a cheap alternative to the gold-standard treatment for intractable chronic pain: interdisciplinary pain-management and rehabilitation programs that involve a team of psychologists, doctors, physical and occupational therapists, and other specialists working with a patient over several weeks at specialized clinics. That approach is far more labor-intensive than taking a pill, but it addresses the "biopsychosocial" nature of chronic pain—the fact that what an individual feels is not wholly determined by the firing of pain nerve fibers but can be affected by mood, personality, social context and even the meaning a person attaches to pain. "If your pain means your cancer is getting worse, it's much less tolerable than if it means you've trained hard for the marathon or you're having a nice baby," observes Mark Sullivan, a psychiatrist at the University of Washington's Center for Pain Relief in Seattle.

Even though opioids were suddenly being prescribed en masse for people with bad back pain and all manner of long-term conditions, most studies had looked only at their effects over six weeks or less. That clearly was not enough time to observe the physical and psychological dependences that develop over months and years or how, as the body habituates to the drugs, people often require higher amounts that raise the risk of respiratory problems, dizziness and life-threatening overdoses.

A few doctors, at the time, were bothered by the knowledge gap. Opioid researcher Erin Krebs was in medical school in the mid-1990s. She remembers being surprised and skeptical that drugs that had never been studied over the long term were being prescribed for months and years at a time. Krebs, now chief of general internal medicine at the Minneapolis VA Health Care System, is researching ways to help the so-called legacy patients of the opioid era manage pain with safer doses. But she is also investigating the more basic question of whether opioids are ever a valid choice for long-term pain. Last year she published the first randomized trial to directly compare opioids with nonopioid painkillers—ranging from popular anti-inflammatories such as ibuprofen to nerve pain drugs such as gabapentin—during a full year. Her team followed 240 patients with moderate to severe back or joint pain and found that, on average, the nonopioid group reported less intense pain and fewer side effects. When she proposed the study in 2010, Krebs says, "the assumption was so strong that opioids were better, some people felt it would be unethical to say some patients couldn't get opioids!"

Krebs has since found further evidence that opioids can be a poor choice for chronic pain. At a 2018 pain conference she presented some shocking preliminary data from a long-term study of 9,245 veterans taking opioids for six months or more. Only a quarter of participants rated the effectiveness of their pain treatment as very good or excellent, and 80.9 percent said that their pain was throughout their body—a symptom that might reflect a suspected drug side effect: a pain syndrome called opioid-induced hyperalgesia. "My initial impression was just wow," Krebs told me. "These people are really sick. We have not fixed these folks."

How to Cut Back

When the risk of opioids seems greater than the benefits—if patients are misusing the drugs or show overdose-related symptoms, for example—the new HHS guidelines urge doctors to consider tapering. The central questions then become how to do that without triggering more agony and desperation and what to offer for pain relief instead. In an ideal world, patients with intractable suffering would go to the interdisciplinary pain and rehabilitation clinics, which have a good track record of switching patients from opioids to other ways of managing pain. But many of these clinics closed when the medical community embraced opioids, and treatment at those that remain is costly. So the search is on for cheaper, practical approaches. In 2018 Darnall published one of the first papers to provide an answer: a very slow, personalized dose reduction.

In a pilot study with 68 patients published in *JAMA Internal Medicine*, Darnall showed that over the course of four months, the 51 individuals who completed the trial were able to cut their opioid dosages nearly in half, on average, without worsening pain. They received careful guidance from a community doctor and a self-help book. A slow reduction was especially critical during the first four weeks, she says, when the dosage was cut by no more than two 5 percent increments. That is considerably less than the 10 percent a week originally suggested in the CDC's 2016 "pocket guide" to tapering opioids and in line with the HHS's updated version.

"If we do these microdose reductions, it allows patients to relax into the process, to gain a sense of trust with their doctor and also with themselves," Darnall explains. "Their number-one concern is increased pain." The goal, she emphasizes, was not to get to zero but to "the lowest comfortable dose." Four participants did manage to taper off completely, she says, "but four people didn't budge or actually increased their dose," and 17 dropped out of the trial. Notably, there was no correlation between a patient's dose at the start of the trial or how long the person had been taking opioids and his or her ability to cut back.

Darnall is eager to determine if additional tools might help more patients succeed in tapering. With funding from the Patient-Centered Outcomes Research Institute (PCORI), an agency created by the 2010 Affordable Care Act, she is now overseeing a one-year trial with 1,365 chronic pain patients called EMPOWER (for Effective Management of Pain and Opioid-Free Ways to Enhance Relief). Five hundred of the patients do not wish to taper and will stick with their current opioid treatment, serving as a control group. The others will be randomly assigned to one of three treatments. One group will simply repeat the methods of Darnall's pilot study. Another will do that regimen plus get eight weekly sessions of group cognitive-behavioral therapy (CBT) for pain, a type of short-term psychological counseling that focuses on changing patterns of thoughts and beliefs to affect behaviors and feelings. The third group will also follow the pilot protocol and add six weekly group workshops on pain "self-management."

Pain self-management is a low-cost intervention led by trained peers rather than health professionals, but it has never been studied in the context of opioid tapering. The method, developed by Stanford health educator Kate Lorig, takes participants through a highly structured series of activities, lessons and discussions that offer tools for managing pain and reclaiming a more active life. At a typical session, patients make weekly "action plans" to do something they have been avoiding because of pain, such as taking a daily walk or cleaning out a closet, and report back on their progress. They learn exercises to warm up achy joints and brainstorm better ways to communicate with doctors. Participants say that being with others who understand chronic pain—including the group leaders— provides inspiration, support and accountability. "You realize that everyone is in a similar boat, and that helps," says Sylvia Nomikos, a retired teacher with severe spinal stenosis, who attended a self-management workshop in Pleasantville, N.Y. Two studies of this type of intervention have found that participants report lasting reductions in pain, disability, depression and health-related anxiety.

Darnall's team will assess how the pain self-management method stacks up against costlier CBT in her EMPOWER study and whether either improves on the basic, slow-tapering protocol. Along the way, they will also collect data on participants' use of marijuana and cannabis products to see what impact they have on opioid reduction, and vice versa. The need for such research is pressing, Darnall says. No matter which interventions come out on top, if the outcomes for any group match or exceed those of her pilot study, she will have demonstrated a safe, practical and economical way to taper opioids that could be carried out in communities everywhere.

Easing Withdrawal

Other researchers, including Sullivan and Krebs, are also testing practical, low-cost ways to help pain patients reduce their reliance on opioids that, if successful, could be scaled up to meet the country's huge need. Krebs is leading a large trial, also funded by PCORI, in which 500 U.S. veterans will work by phone with a pharmacist to optimize the safety and efficacy of their drug regimen. Another 500 will be assigned to a multidisciplinary team (a physician, psychologist and pharmacist or physical therapist) that will put less emphasis on meds as the solution and focus more on achieving personal goals and a better quality of life even if their pain cannot be cured. The study will also look at the usefulness of a medication designed to ease withdrawal.

"No one is required to taper in this study," Krebs points out, but participants who are on high doses of opioids will be educated about their risks. Those who opt to taper will be randomly assigned to do so with or without the help of buprenorphine-naloxone (the generic version of Suboxone), a medication that combines an opioid painkiller with an opioid blocker and provides pain relief, reduces symptoms of withdrawal and has a relatively low risk of overdose. "We know this medication works in the opioid-addiction setting," Krebs explains, "so we're wondering if it could also help people in a pain-treatment context."

The Opioid Reassessment Clinic in West Haven, where Muccino gets treatment, is a site in Krebs's study. Its director, Will Becker, routinely offers buprenorphine-naloxone to patients to help trim their opioid use. About two thirds say yes, Muccino among them. Becker believes the drug provides "a soft landing" to people who have been opioid-dependent for years and years. He also thinks that just presenting patients with choices makes a big difference in their ability to taper: "Having an option empowers them."

Opioid tapering at Becker's clinic emphasizes achieving functional goals defined by patients. These could be returning to work or just getting out of bed earlier. "We try to target SMART goals: specific, measurable, action-oriented, realistic and time-bound," Becker explains. "These are discrete, real things that they can reengage with—things that pain has taken away."

For Muccino, a major goal was to enjoy time with his seven grandkids or, as he put it, "being able to see my grandchildren grow as long as I can—through clean eyes." He regrets missing much of his own kids' childhood: "I was working 60 to 70 hours a week, and I was high on drugs. I'd come home and pass out on the couch." Using buprenorphine-naloxone under Becker's supervision helped him stop taking the OxyContin entirely.

A handful of studies and clinical experience suggest that once patients get past their initial fears, many feel better on lower doses or leaving opiates behind. The underlying pain will not necessarily change, says Stanford's Mackey, but on low doses "what I see is they feel more alive, alert and aware." This is presumably because opiate compounds—including those made in our own bodies—work on several systems in the brain, including those that regulate emotions and attention. "When you flood those systems [with drugs], you get blunted over time." Still, there is a minority of patients who do worse, and pain specialists worry about this group, especially at a time when patients are being pressured to cut back. They point out that not everyone can be weaned or even tapered from opioids, and not everyone should be [see "When to Stick with Opioids" below].

Beyond Opioids

The path away from opioids is going to mean starting fewer patients on them to begin with and making other treatments more accessible—including physical and behavioral therapies and scores of nonopioid medications that are used to fight pain. The first part is easier and already happening: a large study published last year found that first-time opioid prescriptions fell 54 percent between July 2012 and December 2017. What's harder is changing medical practice and patient expectations about what chronic pain treatment looks like. As Sullivan observes, "There's no better way to make your patient happier than to give him some OxyContin, because he feels better in the car on the way home from the pharmacy." Other therapies, he notes, tend to take effect more slowly: "they can make you feel worse before they make you feel better. They can be a lot of work," as is the case with physical or behavioral therapy.

It would help if doctors, especially those in primary care, got better training in how to assess and treat pain, an issue noted by the federal National Pain Strategy released in 2018. (U.S. medical students get only four to 12 hours of instruction on pain, according to a 2011 survey. Veterinarians, by comparison, get 28 hours, Darnall says.) The strategy also points out that "the public at large" would benefit from a better grasp of pain's complexity and how to manage it.

Muccino has gained that understanding. These days, in addition to a low dose of buprenorphine-naloxone, he manages his pain with relaxation, distraction and methods he learned in CBT. At home, he pipes some James Taylor songs through his earbuds, stretches and strengthens with physical therapy exercises. He counts himself lucky to have a supportive family so when the going gets rough, he says, "I play with my grandkids. I go for a ride. Anything but take a pill."

When to Stick with Opioids

While researchers are determining how best to wean pain patients from high-dose opioids, it is quite clear that not everyone can or should cut back. The CDC has explicitly exempted people in pain from cancer or sickle-cell anemia from its cautions about prescribing the drugs. In addition, experts will often hesitate to mess with patients who are living with such profound pain that their lives are balanced on a knife's edge. Andrea Anderson, a patient advocate who was executive director of the Alliance for the Treatment of Intractable Pain, tells story after story of people in extremis—a man who survived 20 minutes of electrocution, a patient who had been engulfed in flames—who depend on large quantities of opioids but who do not dare to taper. No one should be forced to, experts agree.

Clinicians also have seen patients who remain stable and functional on a steady dose, holding down jobs, taking care of their families, not escalating their dosage. "We've got guys who stay on 15- to 20-milligram morphine equivalents [MMEs] for years and do well," says Will Becker, who directs the Opioid Reassessment Clinic at the VA Medical Center in West Haven, Conn., although he concedes that "I've seen a whole lot more who have not stayed on low doses and do poorly."

The thorniest questions arise for patients who are on high doses, continue to struggle with pain and an overall poor quality of life, but do not wish to taper. Often these patients are medically complex, with a variety of physical or psychological conditions that make it difficult to tease apart what portion of their pain is caused by an underlying biological issue, what is the result of drug side effects, and what stems from other ailments that afflict them. "This is where we get into the gray zone," says Sean Mackey, who heads the division of pain medicine at Stanford University. "We need to personalize the approach to each patient and work collaboratively. There is not a one-size-fits-all here."

Not all patients do well with tapering, even if it is done slowly and carefully. Take Nadine Hagl, a 53-year-old army veteran who was referred to Becker's clinic after many years on high-dose Percocet (an oxycodone-acetaminophen combo). Hagl is medically complex in several ways. In addition to painful arthritis that leaves her reliant on a cane, she suffers from PTSD and used to carry 240 pounds on her 5-foot, 1-inch frame before undergoing gastric bypass surgery in 2014 and losing 130 lbs. Her rerouted gut cannot tolerate nonsteroidal anti-inflammatory painkillers, which might otherwise be an alternative to opioids, nor does she respond well to buprenorphine, a medication used to mitigate opioid withdrawal.

Hagl is psychosocially complex, too, given her PTSD diagnosis and the fact that she is the single mom of a son who is on the autism spectrum. Working with Becker's team, Hagl made a good faith effort to try a number of alternatives to opioids, but her pain flared up. They agreed to return her to Percocet, along with an array of nondrug therapies, but specified a lower dose than before and close monitoring.

Pain and addiction specialists agree that patients who remain on long-term opioids should be monitored carefully for side effects and for signs of abuse. All 50 states have prescription-monitoring programs that enable clinicians to detect if a patient is double-dipping with another prescriber and putting themselves at risk.

Given all the pressures to reduce opioid use, it is likely that the number of people taking these drugs long term will continue to dwindle. Mark Sullivan, a pain psychiatrist at the University of Washington, remembers the sparing use of these narcotics that prevailed when he entered the field 30 years ago. "I think we will get to the point where, as it was when I started, opioids are very useful and should be used short term and long term only in exceptional circumstances."

Referenced

Effect of Opioid vs Nonopioid Medications on Pain-Related Function in Patients with Chronic Back Pain or Hip or Knee Osteoarthritis Pain—The SPACE Randomized Clinical Trial. Erin E. Krebs et al. in *Journal of the American Medical Association*, Vol. 319, No. 9, pages 872–882; March 6, 2018.

HHS Guide for Clinicians on the Appropriate Dosage Reduction or Discontinuation of Long-Term Opioid Analgesics. U.S. Department of Health and Human Services, October 2019. Available at www.hhs.gov/opioids/treatment/clinicians-guide-opioid-dosage-reduction/index.html

About the Author

Claudia Wallis, an award-winning journalist, was managing editor of Scientific American Mind.

The Opioid Epidemic Is Surging Among Black People Because of Unequal Access to Treatment

By Melba Newsome and Gioncarlo Valentine

In one way or another, Thomas Gooch has spent more than 30 years struggling with illegal drugs. The 52-year-old Nashville, Tenn., native grew up in extreme poverty. He was first incarcerated in 1988 and spent the next 15 years in and out of jail for using and selling narcotics. "Until 2003," Gooch says. "That was the first time I went to treatment and the last time I used." Since then, for most of 19 years, Gooch has been trying to get others into recovery or just keep them alive. He handed out clean needles and injection-drug equipment—which reduce injuries, infections and overdose deaths—in Nashville's hardest-hit communities. In 2014 he founded My Father's House, a transitional recovery facility for fathers struggling with substance use disorder.

But despite Gooch's long experience, the opioid epidemic recently has brought a level of devastation to the Black community that has shocked him. "I had never seen death the way I've seen death when it comes to opioid addiction," he says. "There's been so many funerals, it doesn't even make sense. I personally know at least 50 to 60 individuals who died from overdoses in the last 10 years." That staggering body count includes Gooch's recently estranged wife in 2020 and a former partner in 2019.

A million people in the U.S. have died of opioid overdoses since the 1990s. But the face—and race—of the opioid epidemic has changed in the past decade. Originally white and middle class, victims are now Black and brown people struggling with long-term addictions and too few resources. During 10 brutal years, opioid and stimulant deaths have increased 575 percent among Black Americans. In 2019 the overall drug overdose death rate among Black people exceeded that of whites for the first time: 36.8 versus

31.6 per 100,000. And with the addition of fentanyl, the synthetic opioid that's 50 to 100 times more powerful than morphine, Black men older than 55 who survived for decades with a heroin addiction are dying at rates four times greater than people of other races in that age group.

The reasons for this dramatic change come down to racial inequities. Research shows that Black people have a harder time getting into treatment programs than white people do, and Black people are less likely to be prescribed the gold standard medications for substance use therapy. "If you are a Black person and have an opioid use disorder, you are likely to receive treatment five years later than if you're a white person," says Nora D. Volkow, director of the National Institute on Drug Abuse at the National Institutes of Health. "Treatments are extraordinarily useful in terms of preventing overdose death so you can actually recover. Five years can make the difference between being alive or not." Black people with substance use problems are afraid of being caught up in a punitive criminal justice system and are less likely to have insurance good enough to allow them to seek help on their own. And the COVID pandemic disrupted many recovery and harm-reduction services, particularly for people of color.

Gooch blames straight-out racial discrimination in the health-care system, too. "When we call different places to try to get people into treatment, the question they ask is 'What drug do they use?'" he recounts with exasperation. "If you say 'crack,' all of a sudden they ain't got no bed available. If you say opioids and heroin, they will find a bed because that's the demographic they want. A couple of times I told patients that the only way they're going to get help is to get drunk and turn themselves into Vanderbilt Hospital because Vanderbilt will hold them for five days, and that'll get them into treatment."

Gooch is one of the people trying to improve access to therapies for addiction and change the overall dysfunctional dynamic. Other groups are bringing more effective addiction treatments within prison walls, reducing the chances of recidivism on release. A proposed federal law would make therapy with the commonly used addiction medication methadone less onerous for an impoverished population, as well as less stigmatizing. And Volkow is using her platform at the NIH to highlight the overwhelming research-based evidence for better ways to understand and treat addiction.

Access to Treatment

The nation's historic reluctance to treat addiction as a health-care issue rather than a criminal justice one has resulted in a health-care system where too few people of any race—just 10 percent—receive treatment for substance use disorder. Several factors, such as stigma and an inability to afford or access care, make the numbers considerably more dismal among people of color. Even after a nonfatal overdose, Black patients are half as likely to be referred to or access treatment as non-Hispanic white patients, according to federal government data.

A growing recognition that criminalization and incarceration do little to curb illegal drug use or improve public health or safety has led to harm-reduction policies such as Good Samaritan laws—statutes that provide limited immunity for low-level drug violations and increase availability of naloxone, a drug that can reverse overdose. But racial disparities have emerged in the application and effectiveness of both measures. A study from RTI International found that Black and Latino intravenous drug users have inequitable access to the medication.

Loftin Wilson, program manager for the NC Harm Reduction Coalition in Durham, N.C., who has worked in the field for more than a decade, says the problems with inequality lead to distrust in the system, which creates a vicious cycle in which people who need help won't go to institutions that can provide help. People entering treatment worry, with good reason, that dealing with the social service system can cause them to lose their employment, housing or even custody of their children. "That's another example of the negative experiences people who use drugs have. They definitely don't land equally on everybody, and people don't experience them all the same way. It is a vastly different experience to be a Black drug user seeking health care than for a white person," Wilson says.

University of Cincinnati psychologist Kathleen Burlew notes, as Volkow does, that when Black patients enter treatment, they are more likely to do so later than white people and are less likely to complete it. In addition to mistrust, she says, the less favorable outcomes result from factors such as clinician bias and lack of racial and ethnic diversity among treatment providers.

Federal resources, such as grants to support local opioid use disorder clinics and programs, also tend to favor white populations. According to 2021 data from the Substance Abuse and Mental Health Services Administration, 77 percent of the clients treated with grant funding were white, 12.9 percent were Black and 2.8 percent were Native American. The disparity is even more pronounced in some states. For example, in 2019 North Carolina announced that white people made up 88 percent of those served by its $54-million federal grant, compared with 7.5 percent for Black people. Native Americans accounted for less than 1 percent of those served.

Medication Inequality

Research has shown that there is a bias among health-care providers against using medication-assisted treatment (MAT), which combines FDA-approved drugs with counseling and behavioral therapies. Substance use specialists consider it the best approach to the opioid use problem. Yet a study published in *JAMA Network* found that about 40 percent of the 368 U.S. residential drug programs surveyed did not offer MAT, and 21 percent actively discouraged people from using it. Many addiction treatment programs are faith-based and see addiction as a moral problem, which leads to the conclusion that relying on medication for abstinence or sobriety simply trades one form of addiction for another. Many general practitioners who lack training in addiction medicine have this misconception.

The three medications approved by the FDA are buprenorphine, methadone and naltrexone. Buprenorphine and methadone are synthetic opioids that block brain opioid receptors and reduce both cravings and withdrawal. Naltrexone is a postdetox monthly injectable that blocks the effects of opioids. Very few insurance providers in the U.S. cover all three medications, and according to the Centers for Disease Control and Prevention, the full range of medications is far less available to Black people.

Research suggests that economics and race influence who receives which medications. Buprenorphine, for instance, is more widely available in counties with predominantly white communities, whereas methadone clinics are usually located in poor communities of color.

To use methadone, patients must make daily visits to a clinic to receive and take the medication under the supervision of a practitioner. This requirement makes it difficult to do things that build a normal life, such as attending school and obtaining and maintaining a job. There is also the stigma of standing in a public line known to everyone passing by as a queue for addiction treatment. "The treatment model was developed [during the Nixon administration] based on racism and a stigmatized view of people with addiction without any thought of privacy or dignity or treating addiction like a health problem," says Andrew Kolodny, medical director of the Opioid Policy Research Collaborative at Brandeis University. The stigma is made worse by methadone's classification as a Schedule II controlled substance, which is defined as a substance with a high potential for abuse, potentially leading to severe psychological or physical dependence. This categorization pushed the medication into a quasicriminalized status and the clinics into minority communities.

Buprenorphine, however, is a completely different story. When opioid use problems increased in white communities, Congress acted to create less stigmatizing treatment options. The Drug Addiction Treatment Act of 2000 ("DATA 2000") lifted an 86-year ban that prevented treating opioid addiction with narcotic medications such as buprenorphine, which today is sold under the brand names Subutex and Suboxone. The majority of doctors who got special federal licenses to prescribe it accept only commercial health insurance and cash, so the drug is usually offered to a more affluent population, which in the U.S. means white people. About 95 percent of buprenorphine patients are white, and 34 percent have private insurance, according to a national study of data through 2015.

John Woodyear is an addiction treatment specialist in Troy, a small rural town in south central North Carolina where the epidemic is exacting an increasingly heavy toll on the Black and Native American populations. Overall overdose death rates increased 40 percent from 2019 to 2020, but death rates among those two groups in particular went up 66 and 93 percent, respectively. Yet Woodyear, who is Black and practices in a town that is 31 percent Black, says his patients are 90 percent white. People come to the clinic through word of mouth or referrals from friends. As long as Woodyear's patients are mostly white, new patients will be mostly white as well, he says.

One exception to this racial pattern is Edwin Chapman's clinic in the Northeast neighborhood of Washington, D.C., one of the district's predominantly Black and most impoverished communities. Chapman, a physician, often prescribes buprenorphine to his patients with opioid use problems, and the overwhelming majority of them are Black. He says that to prescribe the drug, physicians like him must get past certain roadblocks. "The insurance companies in many states put more restrictions on patients in an urban setting, such as requiring prior authorization for addiction treatment," he says. Further, "to increase the dose above 16 or 24 milligrams, you may have to get a prior authorization. The dosing standards were based on the white population and people who were addicted to pills. Our surviving Black population often needs a higher dose of buprenorphine."

Chapman says few physicians in private practice are willing to treat these patients. "They don't really feel comfortable having these patients in their office, or they aren't really prepared to deal with the economic and mental health issues that come with this population," he explains; those disorders include bipolar disorder and schizophrenia, among others.

People have their own biases that keep them away from medication such as buprenorphine, Wilson says. Many view it as simply trading one drug for another. "They think, 'If I'm going to take this step, why not just go to detox and not take any medications at all?'" he says. "There's a big cultural misunderstanding about the fact that [these] medications are the only evidence-based treatment for opioid use disorder. Short-term detox isn't the most appropriate intervention for most people."

Gooch agrees that the bias is real. He facilitates recovery groups at a program operated by a group from Meharry Medical College, a historically Black institution. Yet "I haven't seen one Black person yet," Gooch says. "Some think it's a setup. There's so much distrust, they have a hard time thinking it's legal. It's just the culture of Black people. Many are religious and think [taking the drug] is wrong."

"Those [misconceptions] are holdovers from our having been miseducated from the outset," Chapman says. "Whites have done a tremendous job educating their community that this is a medical problem, a disease. In the African American community, drug addiction has always been and continues to be seen as a moral problem, and incarceration was the treatment."

Hope for Change

In the November 2021 issue of *Neuropsychopharmacology*, Volkow argued that it is long past time for a new approach to drug addiction that would address these misconceptions within the most affected populations and biases among providers. "We have known for decades that addiction is a medical condition—a treatable brain disorder—not a character flaw or a form of social deviance," she wrote.

Volkow argues that treatment reform should start with prison and the criminal justice system. Even though there is no difference along racial lines in who uses illegal drugs, Black people nonetheless were arrested for drug offenses at five times the rate of white people in 2016. The racial disproportionality in incarcerated drug offenders does not reflect higher rates of drug law violations, only higher rates of arrest among racial and ethnic minorities. Currently the number of arrests for heroin (which more Black people use) exceeds the arrests for diverted prescription opioids (which more white people use), even though the latter is more prevalent.

These unequal arrests and incarcerations add to the racial inequalities in drug treatment and survival rates. An estimated two thirds of people in U.S. correctional settings have a diagnosable substance use disorder, and approximately 95 percent will relapse after their release. In the two weeks postrelease, the risk of overdose increases more than 100-fold, and the chances of death increase 12-fold.

Paradoxically, that makes prisons and jails—institutions with the most obvious and overt racial disparities—the places with the greatest potential to bring about effective change. Volkow points to a recent NIH study as proof that starting substance disorder treatment during incarceration lowers the risk of probation violations and reincarcerations and improves the chances of recovery. But only one in 13 prisoners with substance use problems receives treatment, according to a Pew data analysis.

Some local programs have started to tackle some of these issues. In Pittsburgh, the Allegheny Health Network's RIvER (Rethinking Incarceration and Empowering Recovery) Clinic opened in May 2021. Its goal is to reduce recidivism among people with addictions by providing care for the formerly incarcerated immediately on their release from jail, regardless of their ability to pay. Since opening, the clinic's caregivers have engaged with hundreds of people.

New York City recently became the first municipality in the country to sanction overdose prevention centers where people with substance use disorder can use drugs under medical supervision. Two sites, one in East Harlem and the other in Washington Heights, opened in December 2021. They have had more than 10,000 visits and prevented nearly 200 overdoses by administering the medication naloxone.

There are other signs of change, too. California signed a law that requires every treatment provider in the state to provide a "client bill of rights" to notify patients of all aspects of recommended treatment, including no treatment at all, treatment risks and expected results. And federal authorities loosened methadone regulations during the pandemic. Instead of daily in-person visits, more patients were allowed to use telehealth consultations and take doses home. Senators Ed Markey of Massachusetts and Rand Paul of Kentucky have introduced a bill that would make that change permanent. Among other programs and initiatives across the country, these are an indication that drug treatment policy may be headed in a more equitable, evidence-based direction.

About the Authors

Melba Newsome is a 2023 Alicia Patterson fellow, reporting on climate displacement and people of color.

Gioncarlo Valentine is an award-winning photographer and writer from Baltimore. Backed by his seven years of social work experience, Valentine examines issues faced by marginalized populations, most often focusing his lens on the experiences of Black and LGBTQIA+ communities.

Section 4: Treating Addiction

Fighting Back against the Stigma of Addiction

By Nora D. Volkow

U ntreated drug and alcohol use contributes to tens of thousands of deaths every year and affects the lives of many more people. We have effective treatments, including medications for opioid and alcohol use disorders, that could prevent a significant number of these deaths, but they are not being utilized widely enough, and people who could benefit often do not even seek them out. One important reason is the stigma around those with addiction.

Stigma is a problem for people with health conditions ranging from cancer and HIV to a variety of mental illnesses, but it is especially powerful in the context of substance use disorders. Even though medicine long ago reached the consensus that addiction is a complex brain disorder, those with addiction continue to be blamed for their condition. The public, as well as many people working in health care and in the justice system, continues to view addiction as a result of moral weakness and flawed character.

Stigma on the part of health care providers who see patients' drug or alcohol problems as their own fault can lead to substandard care or even to the rejection of individuals seeking treatment. Staff in emergency departments, for instance, may be dismissive of addicted people because they do not view treating drug problems as part of their job. As a result, those showing signs of acute intoxication or withdrawal symptoms are sometimes expelled from the ER by staff who are fearful of their behavior or who assume they are only seeking drugs. People with addiction can internalize this stigma, feeling shame and refusing to seek treatment.

During a visit to Puerto Rico several years ago, I visited a "shooting gallery"—a makeshift injection site—in San Juan, where I met a man who was injecting heroin into his leg. It was severely infected, and I urged him to visit an ER, but he had been treated horribly on previous occasions and preferred risking his life, or probable amputation, to the prospect of repeating his humiliation.

Beyond just impeding the provision or seeking of care, stigma may actually drive addicted people to continue using drugs. Research by Marco Venniro of the National Institute on Drug Abuse has shown that drug-dependent rodents choose social interaction over the drug when given the choice, but when the social choice is punished, the animals revert to drug use. Humans, too, are social beings, and some of us respond to both social and physical punishments by turning to substances to alleviate our pain. The humiliating rejection experienced by those who are stigmatized for their drug use acts as a powerful social punishment, driving them to continue and perhaps intensify their drug taking.

The stigmatization of people with substance use disorders may be even more problematic in the current COVID-19 crisis. In addition to the greater risk associated with homelessness and with drug use itself, the legitimate fear around contagion may mean that bystanders or even first responders will be reluctant to administer lifesaving naloxone to people who have overdosed. And there is a danger that overtaxed hospitals will pass over those with obvious drug problems when making difficult decisions about where to direct limited personnel and resources.

Alleviating stigma is not easy, in part because the rejection of people with addiction or mental illness arises from unease over their violations of social norms. Even health care workers may be at a loss as to how to interact with someone acting threateningly because of withdrawal or because of the effects of certain drugs (for example, PCP) if they have not received training in caring for people with substance use disorders. It is crucial that health care personnel, from staff in emergency departments to physicians, nurses and physician assistants, be trained in caring competently for people with substance use disorders. Treating patients with dignity and compassion is the first step.

There must be wider recognition that susceptibility to the brain changes in addiction is substantially influenced by factors outside an individual's control, such as genetics and the environment in which one is born and raised, and that medical care is often necessary to facilitate recovery as well as to avert the worst outcomes, such as overdose. When people with addiction are stigmatized and rejected, especially by those in health care, it only contributes to the vicious cycle that makes their disease so entrenched.

About the Author

Nora D. Volkow, M.D., is director of the National Institute on Drug Abuse at the National Institutes of Health.

A New Approach to Addiction Treatment

By Jon Morgenstern

T he nation's growing addiction crisis has amplified the urgent and long-standing need for integrating research into the substance abuse treatment and recovery process. While there has been an increase in research activity focused on addiction issues, the challenge is that it often takes a decade or more before important clinical findings can be implemented into real-world care delivery.

How can the industry address this problem and make continuous quality improvement a cornerstone of substance abuse treatment? I believe we need to create addiction treatment learning laboratories that are embedded into, and coexist with, treatment and recovery centers.

The goal of this approach is to accelerate the translation of basic science discoveries into actionable treatment methodologies that can be shared with and help advance the work of addiction professionals nationwide.

Why Now?

While research has generated evidence of treatment efficacy in highly controlled settings, there is limited understanding of how to apply this knowledge in ongoing care regimens. For example, most programs offer a variety of different treatments, but there is no research on the impact of these multicomponent programs or how to tailor care to the unique problems of individual patients.

Additionally, because there is little knowledge of how best to measure progress in treatment, it can be very difficult to make critical decisions about when to extend care or introduce a new treatment. As a result, the current standard of substance use disorder (SUD) treatment too often provides a one-size-fits-all set of services, or if treatment is personalized, it is based on clinical intuition without the benefit of research.

Critical Data

Compared to other areas of health care, the addiction field lags behind in the use and analysis of data. Certainly, the human element can't be replaced, but collecting and analyzing data in a manner that is actionable will help more patients. The need is for real-time data collection to enable care that is tailored to the individual and how he or she changes over time.

For the most part, current SUD treatment programs do not have this capacity as part of routine operations. Consequently, the industry must now begin to work toward developing state-of-the-art clinical informatic platforms that can collect research quality data on every patient at admission, during treatment and for several years following discharge.

The goal is for researchers to be able to identify treatment outcomes and patterns, and in doing so understand the interventions that work best for individual patients. Once best practices along the continuum are identified, clinicians can then integrate them into everyday clinical care.

Bottom line: Being able to see if outcomes improve as treatment is modified will be a significant advancement in the addiction field.

Affiliations and Collaborations

Establishing strong affiliations with the nation's leading health care providers and building collaborative relationships with major research institutions will play an important role in accelerating the integration of research into the substance abuse treatment and recovery process.

A good example of this is how Northwell Health, the largest health care provider in New York, and Engel Burman, a leading developer of assisted-living facilities, have engaged in a joint venture with Wellbridge Addiction Treatment and Research. This unique venture will approach addiction in a modern way by aligning best practices in a manner similar to how Northwell addresses other illnesses like diabetes and cancer.

A key advantage of this venture will be having access to the necessary resources to explore some of the more promising areas of addiction treatment including mapping genetic profiles directly to optimize addiction treatment, as well as expanding research on how genetic biomarkers can inform the use of medications.

Other important areas of study might include imaging, neuroscience, precision medicine and comparative effectiveness. There are huge differences in how patients respond to treatment, which is why integrating research into the treatment process creates a tremendous opportunity to identify more precise markers for determining how a specific patient responds to specific treatments.

Affiliations and collaborations can also help create opportunities to study large cohorts of patients, support continuum of care by tracking patient's recovery, and explore new options for staying in touch with patients over extended periods of time.

Key to all of this will be the ability to leverage the intersection of health care and technology (i.e., "connected health") and apply it to addiction treatment. For example, many of the techniques found effective for other chronic diseases can also be used to promote better management of addiction care.

Drug addiction has now become the deadliest public health crisis in recent U.S. history. To address this major epidemic, it is imperative to find new and innovative approaches to treatment. While having patients down the hall from researchers is very rare in addiction treatment centers, it is now absolutely necessary to study, properly treat and ultimately overcome this devastating disease.

The views expressed are those of the author(s) and are not necessarily those of Scientific American.

About the Author

Jon Morgenstern is an internationally recognized expert on the treatment of substance use disorders. He leads addiction research at Wellbridge Addiction Treatment and Research and serves as assistant vice president of addiction services at Northwell Health.

At Last, Some Help for Meth Addiction

By Claudia Wallis

A decade ago I traveled on assignment to a Rocky Mountain rehab facility where the rich and famous go to dry out and confront their drug habits. It offered every imaginable therapy to its well-heeled clientele and claimed strong results. But I will never forget what the director of operations told me about the clinic's biggest failure: "Our results with meth addicts are dismal," he admitted.

Poor results remain all too typical for what is more formally known as methamphetamine use disorder. About one million people in the U.S. are addicted to meth, a powerful stimulant that—smoked, snorted, injected or swallowed—ruins lives and contributed to more than 12,000 overdose deaths in 2018. Fatal overdoses appear to have spiked by nearly 35 percent during the COVID pandemic. Unlike people battling alcoholism or opioid misuse, meth users have no approved medications to help them shake their habit. And most behavioral therapies fail.

But this tragic picture at last may be changing. A recent study found that a regimen of two medications helped some users stay off the drug. In addition, a psychosocial intervention called contingency management (CM) has been shown to be especially effective and, while not widely available, is now the first-line therapy for people seeking treatment for meth or cocaine addiction within the U.S. Department of Veterans Affairs health system.

All addictions are tough to beat, but methamphetamine poses a particular challenge. A key way that researchers measure the addictive grip of a substance is to look at how much dopamine (a neurotransmitter associated with pleasure) floods into the brain's major reward center during use, based on animal studies. "Methamphetamine is the drug that produces the largest release," says Nora Volkow, director of the National Institute on Drug Abuse. "An animal will go crazy pressing a lever in order to get the drug," she adds. Another metric involves real-world human experience:

When you try a new substance, what is the likelihood of becoming addicted? "In this respect, methamphetamine ranks along with heroin among the top addictive drugs," Volkow says.

The medication study used two substances that target withdrawal. Bupropion, an antidepressant also prescribed for smoking cessation, raises dopamine levels in the brain and thus may buffer the misery of steep drops that occur when people stop using meth. Naltrexone, the second medication, is an opioid blocker that "has an effect on the reward circuit, potentially relieving cravings," explains the study's lead author, Madhukar H. Trivedi, a psychiatrist at the University of Texas Southwestern Medical Center. In a trial with 403 heavy users of meth, a regimen of the two medications helped 13.6 percent stay off the drug, testing meth-free at least three-quarters of the time over a six-week period. Only 2.5 percent of those given placebos achieved that level of abstinence.

Contingency management works on behavior by reinforcing abstinence with prizes. At VA clinics, addicted veterans submit a urine sample twice a week. If the sample is meth-free, they get to pull a slip of paper from a fishbowl. Half the slips show various dollar amounts that can be spent at VA shops, and the rest feature words of encouragement. Two clean samples in a row earn two draws from the fishbowl, three in a row earn three draws, and so on, up to a maximum of eight. But drug-positive urine means no prize. The key "is the immediacy of the reinforcement," says Dominick DePhilippis, a clinical psychologist at the Corporal Michael J. Crescenz VA Medical Center in Philadelphia. That is important, he notes, because the rush of meth is also immediately reinforcing, whether it is the "euphoric feeling that substance use brings or the escape from fatigue or unpleasant mood states" of withdrawal.

A 2018 study with 2,060 VA patients, led by DePhilippis, found that over a 12-week period, participants, on average, showed up for 56 percent of their 24 sessions and that 91 percent of their urine samples were free of the targeted drug. According to a 2018 analysis of 50 trials involving nearly 7,000 patients with meth or cocaine habits, one person benefits from CM for every five treated.

DePhilippis's team is gathering data on CM's long-term efficacy for drug users. If results are good, perhaps more health insurers will overcome concerns about using financial rewards in treatment and cover the therapy. Volkow hopes that meth users will ultimately have a variety of treatments, including some that combine medication with behavioral therapy. That, she says, is how diseases from depression to diabetes are treated. But "we stigmatize addiction," Volkow says, "and insurance is willing to pay much less than for another condition. There's a double standard."

About the Author

Claudia Wallis, an award-winning journalist, was managing editor of Scientific American Mind.

Cannabis Compound Eases Anxiety and Cravings of Heroin Addiction

By Emily Willingham

As anyone who's dealt with substance addiction can tell you, breaking the physical intimacy with the drug isn't always the most challenging part of treatment. People trying to avoid resurrecting their addiction also must grapple with reminders of it: the sights, sounds and people who were part of their addictive behaviors. These cues can trigger a craving for the drug, creating anxiety that steers them straight back into addiction for relief.

The opioid epidemic in the United States has taken more than 300,000 lives, and support for people working to keep these drugs out of their orbit has become crucial. Methadone and buprenorphine, the current medical treatment options, help break the physical craving for opioids by targeting the same pathways that opioids use. Although these drugs can ease physical need, they don't quiet the anxiety that environmental cues can trigger, leaving open a door to addiction reentry.

The cannabis compound cannabidiol (CBD), a nonpsychoactive component of cannabis, might be the key to keeping that door locked. Researchers report that among people with opioid addiction, CBD dampens cue-triggered cravings and anxiety, along with reducing stress hormone levels and heart rate. The results were published May 21, 2019 in the *American Journal of Psychiatry*.

"These findings provide support for an effect of cannabidiol on this process," says Kathryn McHugh, assistant professor in the department of psychiatry at Harvard Medical School's Division of Alcohol and Drug Abuse, who was not involved in the study. However, she cautions, the results are preliminary, and behavioral therapies are also quite effective at dimming the signal from cues.

The anxiety reduction isn't specific to opioid-related cues and could generalize to other situations, says neuroscientist Yasmin

Hurd, first author on the study and director of the Addiction Institute at the Icahn School of Medicine at Mount Sinai. "It's just that this particular anxiety leads someone to take a drug that can cause them death, and anything we can do to decrease that means increasing the precious chance of preventing relapse and saving their lives."

Hurd and her colleagues conducted a randomized, controlled, double-blind trial of 42 drug-abstinent people with a heroin-use disorder. The participants took either 400 or 800 milligrams of CBD or placebo at different intervals so that researchers could assess the immediate and longer-term effects of the compound. Those in the CBD groups exhibited reduced anxiety and craving in response to drug-related cues such as videos showing drug paraphernalia. They also had reduced levels of the stress hormone cortisol in their saliva and lower heart rates. These effects of CBD lasted a week after the last dose, when little to no CBD would be expected to remain in the body.

The antianxiety effects look promising, but whether or not they will generalize is unclear, says Chandni Hindocha, a research fellow in the division of psychiatry, University College London. Pointing to another study showing that a dose of 400 mg of CBD reduced anxiety about public speaking, she says that in both cases, something triggers the anxiety, rather than its being chronic and generalized. "The system on which CBD acts works to bring the body down to a steady state during acute anxiety," Hindocha says, so CBD may have its effects by speeding up that process.

Pinning down the just-right CBD dose may be tricky, says Gustavo González Cuevas, an associate professor and coordinator in the Department of Psychology at the European University of Madrid School of Biomedical and Health Sciences, who was not involved in the study. "Sometimes lower doses of CBD have been proven to be more effective than higher doses," he says.

Dose-finding is a next step, says Hurd, in addition to figuring out the best route, oral or inhaled, for administering a CBD-based drug. One thing is for sure, says Hurd: using commercially available "edibles" or smoking cannabis won't be the best choice because these options offer little dosage control.

About the Author

Emily Willingham is a science writer and author of the books Phallacy: Life Lesson from the Animal Penis *(Avery, Penguin Publishing Group, 2020) and* The Tailored Brain: From Ketamine, to Keto, to Companionship: A User's Guide to Feeling Better and Thinking Smarter *(Basic Books, 2021).*

Could New Weight-Loss Drugs like Ozempic Treat Addiction?

By Sara Reardon

Some users of Ozempic, the popular diabetes drug that can help people eat less and lose weight, have been noticing a welcome side effect. An increasing number of people who use these injections to help control their food cravings say other cravings disappear as well—including ones for nicotine, alcohol, gambling, skin picking and other compulsive behaviors.

The abundance of anecdotal reports has made researchers wonder whether Ozempic and similar weight-loss drugs can serve as a basis for antiaddiction treatments. "It does make a lot of sense," says Lorenzo Leggio, an addiction researcher at the National Institute on Alcohol Abuse and Alcoholism and the National Institute on Drug Abuse. Ozempic, one of the brand names for the drug semaglutide, targets a hormone that tells the body when it is full and, through mechanisms that are not fully understood, weakens the brain's association between food and pleasure. Addiction seems to use similar brain pathways whether it's linked to drugs or alcohol, and animal studies suggest such drugs can help treat it.

But data from human trials are still scarce. Novo Nordisk, which makes Ozempic, and Eli Lilly, which makes a similar medication called Mounjaro and is developing the weight-loss drug candidate retatrutide, nicknamed "triple G," both declined to comment on their respective drugs' potential to treat addiction and said they are not currently running or planning trials to investigate such treatment. So Leggio and other addiction researchers are starting their own studies to directly test whether these drugs, and newer generations of them, will be as safe and effective for treating drug and alcohol addiction as they are for facilitating weight loss. The researchers also want to examine ways to help scientists find out if and how the drugs affect the brain. "People [taking these weight-loss drugs] who may benefit say it's changing their life, but we don't hear from people who don't benefit," Leggio says. "We need the human studies to be done."

How Do the New Weight-Loss Drugs Impact Addictions?

Semaglutide, which was initially developed as a diabetes treatment, is a type of agonist—a substance that binds to specific receptors in the body and prompts a reaction. The drug triggers the pancreas to release a hormone called glucagonlike peptide–1 (GLP-1), which the organ normally produces in response to food. As GLP-1 levels increase, the body registers that it has had enough to eat and reduces hunger cravings as a result. GLP-1 levels can be disrupted in people who are overweight or have diabetes, which causes the body to consume more than it needs instead of recognizing that it is full. By raising hormone levels, semaglutide and similar GLP-1 agonists restore the correct hormone balance, although their effect seems to end if people stop taking the drugs.

Recent evidence suggests that GLP-1 acts on other organ systems as well, including the brain. It's still unclear whether the hormone made in the pancreas enters the brain or if the effect is linked to GLP-1 made in the brain. Either way, the hormone seems to affect the brain's reward pathways and to lower the dopamine levels that make food pleasurable. Dopamine—often called the "feel-good" hormone—also plays a major role in addiction.

Semaglutide's story becomes even more complicated in drug addiction. Addictive drugs such as cocaine and opioids are generally thought to "hijack" the brain's natural reward pathways, says Heath Schmidt, a neuropharmacologist at the University of Pennsylvania. Over time, the brain needs more and more dopamine to function, leading to addiction.

Previous research has found that activating GLP-1 receptors in rats' brain causes the animals to eat less of a high-sugar chow, which they would normally prefer over a less delicious but healthier bland meal when given the option. This suggests that GLP-1 makes unhealthy food less rewarding. Schmidt's team found the same to be true with cocaine: rats that received a GLP-1 agonist took less cocaine when it was offered. The researchers are now repeating the experiments in rats addicted to opioids or fentanyl. Several other studies have shown that GLP-1 agonists cause rats to drink less alcohol and produce less dopamine when they do drink, suggesting that the activity is no longer as pleasurable.

Patricia Sue Grigson, an addiction researcher at Pennsylvania State University, has an alternative explanation: drug seeking is driven not only by pleasurable rewards but also by fear of the bad feelings and physical side effects associated with withdrawal. In this scenario, the brain sees the drug as a physiological need—much like the need for food—and GLP-1 agonists, such as semaglutide, "short-circuit" that association.

Grigson's team is running a clinical trial of a GLP-1 agonist in people receiving treatment for opioid use disorder in a rehabilitation center. As part of the trial, participants taking the medication receive messages throughout the day asking them about their cravings and their mood. The results are expected in a few months. If they indicate improvements in cravings, Grigson says, her team plans to test the drug in a larger group of people who are using opioids but are not in long-term care. It could be used similarly to a medication such as naloxone, which is currently available to treat opioid use disorder. "We're desperate to find something that will give people some relief from their cravings," she says.

Testing Semaglutide for Addiction

Grigson's trial is one of several underway that directly test whether GLP-1 agonists are as effective for addiction in humans as they are in animals. The largest human trial completed so far tested exenatide, an earlier GLP-1 agonist drug that is no longer widely used, in 127 people with alcohol use disorder. People who received exenatide—which works similarly to semaglutide—displayed less activity in the brain's reward centers when shown pictures of alcohol, suggesting that they were less drawn to it. But only participants with obesity ended up drinking significantly less than their peers who received a placebo.

"The results were complex," says Anders Fink-Jensen, a psychiatrist at the University of Copenhagen and senior author of that study. He is unsure why alcohol consumption would only be lowered in people with obesity. But if the study's initial results prove true, that would suggest that the anecdotal reports of "cures" of addictions could be "skewed," Fink-Jensen says, considering that most people who are prescribed a GLP-1 agonist are overweight to begin with.

Fink-Jensen's group is planning to repeat the study exclusively in people with a body mass index (BMI) of more than 30 to determine if the drug is effective at curbing addiction specifically in people with obesity. Leggio and W. Kyle Simmons, a pharmacologist at Oklahoma State University, are also running parallel trials to test semaglutide in people with a range of BMIs to see whether the drug has an effect on alcohol, nicotine and cannabis use over time.

Safety Concerns for Patients with Addiction

GLP-1 agonists have proven to be safe in the general population, but common side effects such as nausea could dissuade people from taking the drugs. And more information is needed on the drugs' safety in people who are recovering from and may also have other health conditions, says Christian Hendershot, a psychiatrist at the University of North Carolina at Chapel Hill who is testing semaglutide on alcohol and nicotine addictions. For example, GLP-1 agonists could be problematic in people who are malnourished from opioid or methamphetamine use, he explains.

Another concern is whether semaglutide might simply be *too* good at dampening pleasure and reward pathways. In her study on opioid use recovery, Grigson is closely monitoring participants' moods and emotions for signs of decreased happiness and motivation in general. Simmons says his team screens participants for depression and suicidal thoughts throughout the trial for the same reason. Animal evidence so far suggests that GLP-1 agonists don't affect overall mood, but the medications might work differently in people who already have mood disorders. Even if such a side effect turns out to be rare, Simmons says, the popularity of Ozempic and similar drugs means that a large number of people could be affected.

Simmons says it's too early to say whether people recovering from addiction would need to take an GLP-1 agonist for the rest of their lives, like people with diabetes do, or whether these drugs could be short-term treatments that curb cravings long enough for people to make lifestyle changes to stay sober. People who stop taking semaglutide for weight loss quickly gain the weight back, and study animals that stop taking it return to alcohol and drug use, but "I don't think we know enough yet" in humans, Simmons says.

Although he is hopeful about the drugs' promise as a treatment for addiction, Hendershot cautions providers against prescribing GLP-1 agonists primarily for drug or alcohol use. The Food and Drug Administration has not approved them for this purpose, but Hendershot says he has already seen some such prescriptions being made. "The anecdotal data has outpaced the science," he says. "It will be some time before we have the trials that are necessary to support using these medications off-label."

About the Author

Sara Reardon is a freelance journalist based in Bozeman, Montana. She is a former staff reporter at Nature, New Scientist *and* Science *and has a master's degree in molecular biology.*

Section 5: Treating Overdoses

Fatal Opioid Overdoses May Be More Common Than Thought

By Jillian Kramer

O pioids have been blamed for the deaths of at least 400,000 U.S. residents in the past two decades—but research now shows that number could be much higher.

Researchers looked at data from the Centers for Disease Control and Prevention on about 630,000 people who died of drug overdoses between 1999 and 2016. They separated the deaths into two categories: those with and without a specific drug indicated.

For the first category, they analyzed how contributing causes of death (such as injuries and heart problems) and personal characteristics (such as age and gender) correlated with opioid involvement. They then used these analyses to calculate the probability of opioid involvement for each unidentified drug overdose, and they found that the number of opioid deaths is likely 28 percent higher than generally reported.

The researchers also noticed that in five states—Alabama, Indiana, Louisiana, Mississippi and Pennsylvania—the number of apparent opioid deaths over the seven-year period more than doubles after taking into account their adjustments.

"Opioid deaths serve as one of the main measures of the opioid crisis, and if opioid deaths are not counted accurately, the extent of the crisis can be severely misrepresented," says Elaine L. Hill, an applied microeconomist at the University of Rochester Medical Center and study co-author. The findings appeared online in February in *Addiction*.

Hill says this research highlights "the potential role of state-level medical examination systems and other policies in driving high rates of underreporting." For instance, a lack of detail in death certificates could relate to whether counties have a coroner or medical examiner, the study authors say. Either can declare cause of death, notes Alina Denham, study co-author and Ph.D. candidate at the University of Rochester. But not all coroners conduct autopsies—so Denham says coroner-based jurisdictions may be more likely to have missing information on particular drugs' involvement in overdoses. Most counties in the five states with the highest discrepancies have coroners.

Robert Anderson, chief of the mortality statistics branch of the National Center for Health Statistics, who was not involved in the study, says the research highlights what his department has known for some time: drugs are often not clearly identified in drug-related deaths, and "there is substantial variability by state and by county in the level of specificity." Because of that, he adds, overdose mortality statistics for opioids—and other drugs—can be misleading. Using calculations like the ones in this study, he says, should help capture more accurate and geographically comparable opioid death estimates.

The researchers say they hope government officials and other researchers will use their new prediction model to calculate estimates for future deaths and to reexamine past data.

About the Author

Jillian Kramer is a freelance journalist currently based in Cleveland, Ohio.

We Need Comprehensive Illicit Drug Analysis Now to Stop Overdose Deaths

By Edward Sisco

The devastating, drug overdose epidemic in the U.S. killed over 105,000 people last year, most from the synthetic opioid fentanyl. But while fentanyl has dominated the headlines, talk in public health circles has shifted to a new illicit drug on the street: xylazine.

Xylazine, also known as "tranq" or "zombie drug," has infiltrated the illicit fentanyl market, generally in the form of a fentanyl-xylazine combination. The nonopioid tranquilizer xylazine likely extends the effects of opioids, bringing new and unique challenges. Commonly used as a veterinary sedative, xylazine can cause injection site wounds that lead to necrosis or amputation.

Its rise spotlights the dynamic and ever-changing nature of the illicit drug market. New substances— bath salts, spice, K2, synthetic cannabinoids and fentanyl analogs—continually appear there, given the ready availability of their chemical precursors, and arising from attempts to skirt laws and regulations, or simply out of consumer preference, with alarming frequency.

In our modern era of illicit synthetic drugs that kill many thousands of Americans every year, we need a new model of warning people about dangerous drugs that tells them the quantity of each drug present in what is sold, including any new substances in these drugs.

At the National Institute of Standards and Technology, where we have created the Rapid Drug Analysis and Research (RaDAR) program, we regularly encounter two or three new substances per month. NPS Discovery, a program run by the Center for Forensic Science Research and Education, identified 137 new substances in the U.S. in the last five years. The European Monitoring Center for

Drugs and Drug Addiction (EMCDDA) identified 370 new substances in Europe in 2020 alone.

Keeping up with changes in the drug supply requires timely and comprehensive data, currently hard to obtain because of a lack of uniform reporting, as well as case backlogs and limitations in technology. Most information comes from three disciplines: forensic drug chemistry, forensic toxicology and public health. Each has different objectives, constraints and workloads that may hinder timely alerts about deadly new drugs.

Forensic drug chemists identify the illegal substances in samples for criminal investigations. Identifying and reporting cutting agents, diluents or substances that are harmful but not illegal, like xylazine, is often not required and may be overlooked in these investigations. Their laboratories also often face large backlogs, prohibiting timely reporting of data. In 2019, the average drug chemistry laboratory in the United States had a backlog of 1,862 cases and it took 60 days for a case to be analyzed and results reported.

Forensic toxicologists determine if a person was under the influence of drugs or determine what drugs lead to an overdose. They often rely on testing that uses drug panels—targeted lists of commonly abused drugs—which inhibits the discovery of new substances. Their laboratories also face backlogs.

In public health, the goal is to inform people what is in a baggie or pill before they consume it. This community relies heavily on immunoassay fentanyl test strips that can detect the presence of fentanyl (and some of its analogues) only. Fourier transform infrared spectroscopy (FTIR) is also heavily used in this setting but can only detect the major components of mixtures—likely missing the minor, potentially toxic substances.

Overcoming these constraints to get closer to real-time, comprehensive testing is possible, but it will require rethinking the disciplines and increasing their collaboration. Several ongoing efforts, such as is NIST's RaDAR program, show this is possible. Through this program, I and other chemists provide same-day analysis and comprehensive reporting of drug paraphernalia residues from syringe service programs, overdose scenes or police seizures to public health and public safety entities. This has enabled detection of new substances within a day of a sample being collected. These partnerships have revealed that people who use drugs are often unaware of all the substances present in what they use. Informed use—telling people just what is really in their pills or powder—through the RaDAR program and others like it, has motivated behavioral changes, and better outcomes, in people who use drugs.

To truly unlock comprehensive testing, however, we need to also reconsider our analytical approaches and how we are using the data. While identifying what dangerous substances are in the supply remains vital, knowing its quantity is also important in providing insight into potency and whether bad batches of drugs are on the street. Quantitation has long been completed in biological fluids for toxicological analyses to help determine impairment or cause of death, but it is rarely employed in drug chemistry or public health, when critical information about the actual powder or pill could be obtained. Luckily, the instrumentation and analyses used by toxicologists can be easily adapted and employed in the other two disciplines.

Identifying new substances would be another huge step in unlocking comprehensive testing. Current instruments and methods rely on libraries or databases of known compounds to make identifications, which means it is easy to detect things we know to look for, but difficult to identify new ones. By using machine learning or other algorithms to examine the data produced by these instruments, researchers could identify new substances where no library entry exists. Though early, this is likely only a matter of time before its widespread use in all three disciplines.

While we wait for a mythical low-cost, on-site, rapid technology that can qualitatively and quantitatively identify all chemicals in a drug sample, we need to focus on rethinking the use of the technologies we already have, to comprehensively investigate the drug supply. Modifying methods, promoting data sharing, unifying reporting and emphasizing rapid analysis could go a long way.

Just as we warn people about tainted lettuce or contaminated eye drops, we need to warn them about dangerous adulterants or new drugs in an illicit drug supply already killing hundreds of Americans every day. It is past time to become more proactive in our approach. No longer is it a question of whether there will be a new drug on the street but instead a question of when. And the unfortunate answer is that it is likely already here; we just haven't found it yet.

This is an opinion and analysis article, and the views expressed by the author or authors are not necessarily those of Scientific American.

About the Author

Edward Sisco is a research chemist at the National Institute of Standards and Technology whose work focuses on developing new methods for illicit drug detection and analysis. He is also the lead on the RaDAR project, seeking to provide near real-time monitoring of the illicit drug supply. The opinions expressed here are those of the author and do not necessarily represent the views of NIST.

How Over-the-Counter Narcan Can Help Reverse Opioid Overdoses

By Meghan Bartels

A lifesaving drug that can reverse an opioid overdose will be available on pharmacy shelves without a prescription this summer, a regulatory relaxation that experts herald as an important step in managing the U.S. opioid epidemic.

Currently, naloxone is officially classified as prescription-only but is also available from pharmacists in states with a standing order—a directive designed to increase access to public health interventions such as annual flu shots—or a similar protocol. At participating pharmacies, an individual doesn't need a prescription with their name on it to access naloxone but does need to speak with a pharmacist in person.

The Food and Drug Administration announced on March 29, 2023 that it had approved Narcan, a nasal spray containing the opioid-overdose-stopping drug naloxone, for distribution over the counter in the retail sections of pharmacies like a typical cough medicine or painkiller. In a statement at that time, Emergent BioSolutions, a company headquartered in Maryland that manufactures Narcan, said it expected the medication would hit shelves by late summer, although the drug's retail price is not yet known.

The move comes as the opioid death toll continues to rise. According to the National Institutes of Health, more than 80,000 people in the U.S. died from an opioid overdose in 2021.

"We really need to do everything we possibly can to make a dent in the overdose death crisis here in the U.S.," says Kimberly Sue, an assistant professor of medicine at the Yale University School of Medicine.

Scientific American spoke to some experts in harm reduction and opioid use disorder about what the FDA's decision means, how naloxone works and what role it can play in stemming the crisis.

Q: How does naloxone work?

A: During an overdose, molecules of opioids such as heroin, morphine or fentanyl bind to structures called mu opioid receptors throughout the body—especially those in the brain and gut. When enough opioid molecules bind to receptors in the brain, breathing begins to shut down.

Naloxone binds to those same receptors more strongly than opioids do, so it can physically knock opioids away from the receptors and stop an overdose in its tracks. And even though naloxone binds to the same receptors, it doesn't produce the same effects—so it doesn't cause a euphoric "high" like opioids do. The process isn't foolproof: it might take multiple doses for naloxone to kick in, and its effect only lasts about half an hour. As it wears off, an overdose can resume—but naloxone buys crucial time to get medical help.

Naloxone can be administered intravenously in medical settings. Narcan, one nasal spray version, will be available over the counter under the new FDA approval. Another brand of nasal spray, Kloxxado, will continue to require a prescription.

Q: What are the symptoms of an opioid overdose, and how is naloxone spray administered?

A: The two key symptoms of an opioid overdose are difficulty breathing and nonresponsiveness. A person's skin can also become discolored, and the pupils of the eyes sometimes shrink to pinpricks.

Naloxone nasal spray is relatively simple to administer: insert the tip of the nozzle into one nostril and push the plunger in. If it turns out that someone doesn't have opioids in their system, the procedure is still safe because naloxone only binds to mu opioid receptors. "We don't have to worry about causing them harm if, for some reason, it's not an overdose," says Laura Palombi, a public health pharmacist at the University of Minnesota, who specializes in harm reduction—an approach that aims to reduce the dangers of drug use in a compassionate and nonjudgmental way.

After administering naloxone, call 911 and either perform rescue breathing if possible or turn the person on their side to reduce the risk of choking. If symptoms don't subside within a few minutes, additional doses in alternating nostrils may be needed to stop the overdose. Palombi says she's heard of cases requiring as many as eight sprays.

Harm reduction experts emphasize that naloxone will only counteract an opioid overdose. If someone is under the influence of alcohol or a different class of drug, this antidote won't help. If a person has multiple drugs in their system, naloxone will only reverse the opioid overdose. "I would say definitely take a training on how to administer [Narcan]," says Allie McDevitt, a recovery case manager at Life House, a youth shelter in Minnesota. She used five doses of the drug to help someone who went into overdose near the organization. "It's tough because until you've actually been in the situation, like many things, it's easier said than done," McDevitt says.

Q: How will making naloxone available over the counter help people?

A: Naloxone is currently available only from pharmacists and through community harm reduction centers or similar programs. The FDA's decision means this medication can also be sold online and at a range of stores, making it far more accessible to the public.

That's important, experts say, because people who struggle with addiction-related shame can be reluctant to speak with a medical provider about getting naloxone. "I would say that stigma is our number one barrier to getting naloxone out in the community," Palombi says. She hopes the move to make this medication available over the counter will also show people that it is safe. "All of us should have it in our household as a part of our first aid kit," she says.

But experts still have a lot of questions about how the move will play out, especially in terms of cost. Estimates vary, but

Palombi says the best price she can find now is still nearly $50 for a box of two Narcan doses—which is steep, considering that a single overdose may require several dispensers. Some health insurance programs currently cover naloxone, but they usually don't cover over-the-counter medications.

Whether the price tag will shrink once the medicine no longer requires a prescription isn't yet clear. "There have been examples where, when things move to [over the counter], it actually becomes in some ways more expensive," says Jonathan Watanabe, a clinical pharmacist at the University of California, Irvine.

Sue also notes concerns about the price and says structural inequalities make plenty of her patients unable to afford even a $3 copay. "This will not solve getting it in the hands of people who are most vulnerable to overdose," she says.

Palombi says community harm reduction centers may remain the best places for people on tight budgets to get naloxone because these organizations sometimes receive grants to help distribute the medication.

But Kavita Babu, a medical toxicologist at the University of Massachusetts Chan Medical School, worries that lowering regulatory hurdles may actually disadvantage such organizations. "What you never want to hear is that because naloxone is now available over the counter, the funding for naloxone distribution programs has been reduced," she says. Like others, Babu describes the FDA's move as incremental progress. "Over the counter is better than prescription; free is better than over the counter," she says.

Q: Will naloxone alone be enough?

A: Some in the field say the opioid crisis in the U.S. will require a lot more than naloxone to tackle—and that this would be the case even if the drug was easier and cheaper to get.

"This is a really important step, but it's not all the way to the goal line," says Watanabe, who directs the U.C. Irvine

Center for Data-Driven Drugs Research and Policy. In addition to addressing the economics of naloxone access, he has called for better access to buprenorphine and methadone, long-term medications that treat opioid use disorder.

Even before the decision to sell it over the counter, "we've given away naloxone like candy for the last several years, and opioid death rates have continued to rise," says Edward Boyer, a medical toxicologist at the Ohio State University Wexner Medical Center. Emergent BioSolutions says 44 million doses of Narcan have been distributed since 2016, when it first became available. But opioid overdose deaths have nearly doubled since then. Some 47,000 people died of such an overdose in 2017, compared with 80,000 in 2021, according to the National Institutes of Health.

Babu blames that rise on fentanyl, a synthetic opioid that's much stronger than morphine or heroin and is often mixed into other drugs, catching people unaware. "I hate to think about what these numbers could look like without the programs that are currently in place and the energy and thought and funding that're being put into preventing overdose deaths," she says.

Sue emphasizes that behind all these numbers are real people. "Those are our family, our friends, our community, our patients," she says. "Every opioid overdose death is a policy failure."

About the Author

Meghan Bartels is a science journalist based in New York City. She joined Scientific American *in 2023 and is now a senior news reporter. Previously, she spent more than four years as a writer and editor at Space.com, as well as nearly a year as a science reporter at Newsweek, where she focused on space and Earth science. Her writing has also appeared in Audubon, Nautilus, Astronomy and Smithsonian, among other publications. She attended Georgetown University and earned a master's in journalism at New York University's Science, Health and Environmental Reporting Program.*

To Treat Overdose Patients Now, Hospitals Must Test for More Kinds of Drugs

By Erin Artigiani, Amy Billing and Eric D. Wish

Hospitals link people to treatment in their time of greatest need. That includes drug overdoses, which now kill more than 100,000 people in the U.S. every year.

However, the standard hospital urine drug tests often do not detect fentanyl, which today is the leading cause of fatal overdoses, or other "synthetic" substances. Expanded urinalyses that could detect them can be time-consuming and cost-prohibitive.

But if hospital drug screens fail to detect these drugs, people will likely not be fully diagnosed. Without an opioid-positive urine test, they may not be accepted into an opioid treatment program. Or their treatment may not be covered by insurance. Without clear identification of all the substances involved in their visit, patients may be less likely to remain in treatment, even if they are accepted.

Most hospitals, however, are still testing for the drugs driving previous drug crises, such as heroin and cocaine, and have little concrete data about the drugs to which their patients are now being exposed. In fact, in the second quarter of 2022, only 5 percent of hospitals included fentanyl in their standard drug screen. One year later, this percentage had only increased to approximately 14 percent, while testing for opiates (natural opioids like heroin) remained at about 50 percent. That's a decade into an overdose crisis driven by fentanyl that has claimed more than a million American lives.

The overdose crisis is in constant flux, and users are often unaware of the drugs to which they have been exposed. Changes in drug composition can alter the symptoms seen in emergency departments and can change patients' treatment needs. Drug use and overdose are often very individualized. Therefore, America's hospitals must have access to expanded urinalyses to understand all the drugs to which their patients have been exposed.

The University of Maryland's Center for Substance Use, Addiction, and Health Research (CESAR), where we work, has been piloting a new approach, the Emergency Department Drug Surveillance (EDDS) system, with federal and state funding. We currently offer 50 hospitals across the U.S. the opportunity to submit anonymous urine specimens at no cost to the hospitals for expanded urinalyses. We look for many more substances than local hospitals can routinely test for; we use the results to identify patient exposure to specific drugs and to track new patterns of drug use that may be emerging in the population.

Our program could serve as the first phase of a national system to inform hospitals about the drugs to which their patients have been exposed, as well as the role of multiple drugs, or polysubstance use, in overdoses. Hospitals have already used our findings to update their urine drug test panels. For example, EDDS has documented patient exposure to drugs such as fentanyl and xylazine across the U.S. Two hospitals in Baltimore added fentanyl to their standard drug screens in 2019 after participating in EDDS and have since found fentanyl to be the most frequently detected drug in 70 percent or more of specimens tested each year.

In addition, California and Maryland have passed legislation requiring all of their hospitals to include fentanyl in urine drug screens to diagnose patient drug exposure. This is an important step, but as we stressed earlier, illicit drugs are constantly changing. EDDS was able, for example, to detect the animal tranquilizer xylazine in urine specimens from hospitals in Florida, Georgia, South Carolina, Tennessee and Maryland. The drug most likely to be found in addition to xylazine was fentanyl, detected in 85 percent of the xylazine-positive specimens. Xylazine can worsen the life-threatening effects of opioids by causing dangerously slowed breathing and low blood pressure.

EDDS researchers believe that it is essential to launch a true nationwide system to provide hospitals with expanded urine testing at regular intervals and support physicians interested in conducting more in-depth research. We now have a proven method for doing this. More states should follow the lead taken by California and Maryland and require every hospital to include fentanyl in diagnostic drug screens. New drugs such as xylazine should also be added to urine drug screens in states where they are an identified part of the illicit drug market.

Most specimens positive for drugs such as fentanyl and xylazine are also positive for at least one other drug on standard hospital urine screens. While these results may provide adequate information for physicians to treat the immediate medical condition, they don't ensure that hospitals can link patients to the substance use treatment they need to start a successful recovery. The EDDS system has laid the foundation for a nationwide system, but more work still needs to be done.

With nearly 300 Americans a day dying of overdoses and a nonfatal opioid overdose occurring approximately every three minutes, it is imperative that a system for collaborating with hospitals to conduct expanded urinalyses be fully funded by the federal government. A centralized system like this can regularly collect drug use information that can then be disseminated in a practical and useful manner, and support work with local physicians to conduct more in-depth research, as well as inform health policy. Other tools, such as urine test strips for xylazine and fentanyl, could also support a cost-effective approach to expanding hospital testing abilities and monitoring drug use trends.

Without these kinds of resources, we will forever play catch-up, striving to identify emerging drugs and keep up with the illicit drug market. And patients will continue to miss opportunities for treatment and recovery.

This is an opinion and analysis article, and the views expressed by the author or authors are not necessarily those of Scientific American.

The views presented here are those of the authors and do not necessarily represent the official views of the CESAR funding agencies, any other federal or state of Maryland agencies, or the participating hospitals.

About the Authors

Erin Artigiani is deputy director for policy at CESAR at the University of Maryland and co-investigator on the EDDS system. She received an MA in Sociology from UCLA in 1991.

Amy Billing is the project manager for the EDDS system at CESAR. She received an MSSA from Case Western Reserve University in 2001.

Eric D. Wish is the founding director of CESAR and is currently the principal investigator of the EDDS system. He received his Ph.D. in psychology from Washington University in St. Louis in 1977.

GLOSSARY

chronic Occurring constantly or repeatedly over a long period of time; habitual, regular.

decriminalization The removal of criminal penalties, such as for drug possession or use, while still keeping it under some form of regulation.

Diagnostic and Statistical Manual A publication from the American Psychiatric Association widely recognized as an authority on the classification, diagnosis, and treatment of mental disorders.

holistic Analysis or treatment of a medical condition not in isolation but as part of the entirety of a person's physical, social, and emotional life.

medicalization Treatment or view of a condition or symptom as medical in nature, rather than social or environmental.

neuroplasticity The ability of networks of neurons in the brain to grow and reorganize so that they function in different ways.

neuroscientist Person who studies the physiology, biochemistry, and behavior of nerve cells and tissues.

recidivism Tendency to relapse into a previous state, condition, or pattern of behavior.

remission Reduction or moderation of symptoms of an illness or condition.

taper Used in medical terminology, to gradually reduce one's dependence on an addictive substance.

withdrawal Physical and psychological symptoms that arise during or after the discontinuation of the use of an addictive substance.

FURTHER INFORMATION

Caulkins, Jonathan, and Peter Reuter. "Stopping Fentanyl at the Border Won't Work. We Must Reimagine Drug Law Enforcement," *Scientific American,* April 17, 2023, https://www.scientificamerican.com/article/stopping-fentanyl-at-the-border-wont-work-we-must-reimagine-drug-law-enforcement/.

Greenspan, Jessie. "Is Marijuana Bad for Health? Here's What We Know So Far," *Scientific American,* March 1, 2024, https://www.scientificamerican.com/article/is-marijuana-bad-for-health-heres-what-we-know-so-far/.

Hafner, Katie, Carol Sutton Lewis, and the Lost Women of Science Initiative. "A New Era in Addiction Medicine: A Trailblazing Doctor's Legacy and the Ongoing Search for a Cure," *Scientific American,* May 4, 2023, https://www.scientificamerican.com/article/a-new-era-in-addiction-medicine-a-trailblazing-doctors-legacy-and-the-ongoing-search-for-a-cure/.

Russell, Erin. "Over-the-Counter Narcan Is a Small Win in the Overdose Crisis," *Scientific American,* April 21, 2023. https://www.scientificamerican.com/article/over-the-counter-narcan-is-a-small-win-in-the-overdose-crisis-we-need-more/.

Szalavitz, Maia. "Vivitrol, Used to Fight Opioid Misuse, Has a Major Overdose Problem," *Scientific American,* September 13, 2023, https://www.scientificamerican.com/article/vivitrol-used-to-fight-opioid-misuse-has-a-major-overdose-problem/.

White, C. Michael. "'Gas Station Heroin' Is a Dangerous and Often Contaminated Supplement," *Scientific American,* February 6, 2024, https://www.scientificamerican.com/article/gas-station-heroin-is-a-dangerous-and-often-contaminated-supplement/.

Young, Lauren J. "New Drug for Cannabis Use Disorder Shows Promise in Early Trials in Humans," *Scientific American,* June 21, 2023, https://www.scientificamerican.com/article/new-drug-for-cannabis-use-disorder-shows-promise-in-early-trials-in-humans/.

CITATIONS

1.1 Is Addiction a Disease? by Elly Vintiadis (November 8, 2017); 1.2 Food, Sex, Gambling, the Internet: When Is It Addiction? by Carl Erik Fisher (January 1, 2016); 1.3 What Does It Mean When We Call Addiction a Brain Disorder? by Nora D. Volkow (March 23, 2018); 1.4 Scientists Spot Addiction-Associated Circuit in Rats by Simon Makin (January 1, 2020); 1.5 Recent Research Sheds New Light on Why Nicotine Is So Addictive by Nora D. Volkow (September 28, 2018); 2.1 Marie Nyswander Changed the Landscape of Addiction. Here's How Her Story Begins by Katie Hafner, Carol Sutton Lewis & The Lost Women Of Science Initiative (March 30, 2023); 2.2 These Doctors Fought the Federal Bureau of Narcotics to Treat Addiction—With Drugs by Katie Hafner, Carol Sutton Lewis & The Lost Women Of Science Initiative (April 13, 2023); 2.3 Methadone Maintenance versus Synthetic Heaven by Katie Hafner, Carol Sutton Lewis & The Lost Women Of Science Initiative (April 20, 2023); 3.1 Against Medical Advice: Another Deadly Consequence of Our Opioid Epidemic by Zoe Adams (February 19, 2024); 3.2 We're Overlooking a Major Culprit in the Opioid Crisis by Maia Szalavitz (May 28, 2021); 3.3 How to Break the Bonds of Opioids by Claudia Wallis (January 1, 2020); 3.4 The Opioid Epidemic Is Surging among Black People because of Unequal Access to Treatment by Melba Newsome & Gioncarlo Valentine (December 1, 2022); 4.1 Fighting Back against the Stigma of Addiction by Nora D. Volkow (September 1, 2020); 4.2 A New Approach to Addiction Treatment by Jon Morgenstern (June 4, 2019); 4.3 At Last, Some Help for Meth Addiction by Claudia Wallis (April 1, 2021); 4.4 Cannabis Compound Eases Anxiety and Cravings of Heroin Addiction by Emily Willingham (May 21, 2019); 4.5 Could New Weight-Loss Drugs like Ozempic Treat Addiction? by Sara Reardon (July 12, 2023); 5.1 Fatal Opioid Overdoses May Be More Common Than Thought by Jillian Kramer (June 1, 2020); 5.2 We Need Comprehensive Illicit Drug Analysis Now to Stop Overdose Deaths by Edward Sisco (August 22, 2023); 5.3 How Over-the-Counter Narcan Can Help Reverse Opioid Overdoses by Meghan Bartels (April 11, 2023); 5.4 To Treat Overdose Patients Now, Hospitals Must Test for More Kinds of Drugs by Erin Artigiani, Amy Billing & Eric D. Wish (November 15, 2023).

Each author biography was accurate at the time the article was originally published.

INDEX